Entering this book is like walking into one of those second-hand bookstores where the books are piled to the ceiling and each stack obscures another stack behind it and you are struck, once your eyes adjust to the dusty light, with the vertigo of being at the edge of the infinite; Melville is here, and Keats and Dickinson and Simonides and Leibniz and Dante and Hölderlin, as well as a dozen seductively arcane volumes on cryptography and God and *trompe l'oeil*. Or it's like entering an abandoned Baroque ballroom in which a thousand mirrored tops spin, making the gilt surfaces flash in every direction, so that for a moment you feel suspended from the ceiling. Or it's like driving across America in an old car, watching the actual weather unfold outside your window, and talking all night with your companion, a poet-essayist whose talk is a kind of music you stay awake to hear, who has in his pocket the keys to a secondhand bookstore and a secret ballroom where, years ago, he set a thousand tops spinning on the floor.

Kristen Case, author of *Principles of Economics*,
editor of *21/19: Contemporary Poets in the 19th Century Archive*

Incryptions

Kylan Rice

Spuyten Duyvil
New York City

© 2021 Kylan Rice
ISBN 978-1-952419-64-5

Library of Congress Cataloging-in-Publication Data

Names: Rice, Kylan, author.
Title: Incryptions / Kylan Rice.
Description: New York City : Spuyten Duyvil, [2021] |
Identifiers: LCCN 2021002103 | ISBN 9781952419645 (paperback)
Subjects: LCGFT: Essays.
Classification: LCC PS3618.I2996 I57 2021 | DDC 814/.6--dc23
LC record available at https://lccn.loc.gov/2021002103

for Dan Beachy-Quick

Contents

Work for the Dead	1
Encryption	10
Fire or Lime	18
E	24
Concrete	30
This Land Was Made	34
Haul	40
Likes	45
Cognoscenti in a Room Hung with Pictures	53
Wolf Interval	63
Cryptography	67
Bees	83
A Simple Life	91
Gnats	101
A Perfect Summer Life	111

Work for the Dead

I only remember his hands. Or maybe I remember an assembly of hands belonging to many men, all averaged together, having been gripped and gripped my whole life in familiar ceremonies like this one. Sometimes by the wrist, sometimes the shoulder, sometimes as they came to rest on top of my head to bless me. Always these hands are warm and blotched and broad, used to manipulating machinery or wood. Age has made them uncertain, shaky in reaching out, but when they get ahold of me, they become firm and assured.

With his hands or a composite of hands upon me, and drops of holy oil in my hair, I am given a new name. He tells me that it is a password, and that at the veil of judgment after death, someone will ask me for this name. If I remember it, and if I have kept it utterly secret for all of my mortal days, I will be able to pass over into paradise.

Though I myself have only the one new name, I have performed the same initiatory naming ritual many times, not on my behalf but for the dead. On each occasion I am given a scrap of blue paper to take into a small, unadorned room of the temple with the name of a stranger printed on it, long deceased, sometimes for hundreds of years, and in this room I am given a new name for them, to carry with me through other chambers as I complete additional rituals by proxy. Often the new name is written on the slip of paper in a blunt red pencil, in case I forget it at the crucial moment, when I have to whisper it through a veil in order to be able to step through into a bright, white space embossed with gold and full of cream-upholstered hardwood furniture where people can sit and meditate in silence—this final room the culmination of a ritual that must be completed physically in this life by anyone who wishes to secure glory in the next. In addition to the name, there are other phrases and statements I have to remember to speak along the way. If I forget these, there are elderly helpers dressed in white to murmur me my lines. When living Mormons do this "work for the dead," they offer up their bodies for an hour or two to those who died before they were able to perform the necessary ceremonies for themselves.

On the internet you can find a list of new names typically given in the temple. One Reddit member reports that there were only two names in the church's early history—Abraham for men, Sarah for women—but this had a depersonalizing effect, a password stripped of its singular jeopardy, its hash or hex of special characters, as unspeakable as unpronounceable, shibboleth or *shibbólet,* Hebrew for an ear of wheat. Neither name a seed that's truly awkward on the tongue, that presses me to whisper it. Perhaps to introduce more urgency or risk, Abraham and Sarah were multiplied eventually into a family, an expanded list of names from the Bible, like Boaz and Ephraim, Huldah and Abish, plus more common, Anglo-European assignations mixed in, too, like Frederick, Julia, Norma, and Margaret.

The new name is one of several coded signs given in the temple. All of these "tokens" are given under strict, even menacing conditions: you are forbidden to share signs or their names with the uninitiated, or risk eternal punishment. Though no longer part of the modern temple ceremony, the sign-giving portion used to require that initiates make gestures of self-disembowelment as a way to promise never to share sacred secrets. Part of the ritual today continues to dramatize and warn against the temptation to sell the signs for money. I guess writing about them is a version of this, a form of selling out. When I lived in Provo, Utah, the only coffee shop in town sometimes had flyers pinned up on cork-board to advertise shows by local black metal bands named after certain of the secret, unsharable temple tokens. This public form of desecration and self-damnation somehow, in the context of their music, the opposite of selling out. A display of Satanic commitment.

Short of that, how close to the veil can I bring you? How much can I tell you without damning myself?

Not my name, certainly. Even saying how I came by it is risk, I think. But what exactly am I risking at this point, now that the faith that animates these signs and the bans they come with has drained away and left behind the dry ground of this world, and this world only? There is, of course, the knowledge that these rituals are sacred still to family, to people close to me, and that to write about them is to bring them embarrassment and shame. Less to risk heaven, then, than love.

But the name is perfect. I mean, if I told you, you would understand why I needed to. I mean that its origins, the Bible story it is connected with would explain so much, would help you understand why I am writing at all, one narrative shedding light on another. This impulse, then, to tell you my name a form of apology—meaning, originally, etymologically, a reason for speaking. *Apó* in Greek signifying "from" as in "because of" or "after"; *logos*, meaning "speech." To speak after, before. An apology, in the case of Socrates anyway, is even more specifically a defense, a response to an attack, an aftermath. The reason for my speaking is whatever has come before me, and called me out, compelled me.

What has come before me is an ancient story connected with a name I cannot tell you, or risk a loss of love, which is to say damnation. As with Greek tragedy, the action happens off-stage, the attack takes place behind a veil, a chorus hastens to tell you, to have you share in their confusion.

Instead, to apologize for apologizing. Or nearly. Because I won't give it to you, my name which is not mine, belonging to a figure out of scripture. Or if I do, it will be in a whisper, from the corner of my mouth. If anything, an indirection.

For the way is not straight.

One morning in early fall of 1824, not far from the Erie Canal in upstate New York, a farmer and some of his neighbors dug up the dead body of his oldest son to prove to the local townspeople that it was still intact, undissected. A rumor was going around that parts of the body had been cut away and used by one of the farmer's younger sons to perform necromancy in order to recover buried treasure guarded over by an angel. The farmer paid for a notice in a local newspaper to insist publicly that the rumor was false, describing how he had "repaired to the grave, and removing the earth, found the body, which had not been disturbed." To disturb as a means of proving nothing is disturbed, that nothing is wrong.

See, the secret is safe. The cryptic undecrypted.

The farmer's younger son, Joseph Smith Jr., the future founder of the Mormon church, had for two years been attempting to recover the treasure. Upon their retrieval, a set of gold plates etched with strange hieroglyphics were decoded with seer-stones, polished rocks used as scrying devices. Decrypted from the earth and translated, the text would be published as the *Book of Mormon*, advertised as a supplement to the Bible, an account of Christianity as it emerged organically on the American continent, probably somewhere near the Yucatán peninsula, parallel with its spread throughout

Syria, Europe, Anatolia, Mesopotamia, Transcaucasia, Egypt, and Ethiopia. The literary critic Harold Bloom once called Mormonism the American religion, probably because it so emphatically shifts emphasis from the Old World to the New. But Mormonism might also qualify for Bloom's epithet because it has institutionalized a massive global missionary program, exporting a religion rooted in the American hemisphere. In addition, the new religion's nineteenth-century epicenters tracked with Manifest Destiny and the westward push by pioneers.

But before any of this could happen, Smith had to obtain the buried plates. In 1823, on a hill beneath which the treasure apparently lay, the guardian angel informed Smith that he couldn't take the plates yet, and that he had to return the following year with the "right person" in order to do so. Intuiting that the "right person" was his older brother Alvin, Smith must have despaired for reasons more than brotherly love when Alvin died of mercury poisoning less than a month after the angel made its decree. When town gossips learned that the young treasure-seeker had intended to bring Alvin on his next expedition, they must have assumed that Smith would try the next best thing in order to obey the otherworldly guardian: exhume and haul his brother's body, or pieces of it, to the moonlit hill. Some scholars explain that this assumption was founded in magical and necromantic texts that may have been available in Upper New York during the Second Great Awakening, a period of intense spiritual fervor, when treasure-hunting by occult means was common practice. "From hence it is," says pseudo-Agrippa in his fourth *Book of Occult Philosophy*, "that the Souls of the dead are not to be called up without blood, or by the application of some part of their relict Body."

Some forty years after the rumored exhumation, soon following the Civil War, the beloved American poet John Greenleaf Whittier published a long poem, "Snow-Bound: A Winter Idyll," which became a major popular success, narrating the intimate, fireside activities of a family trapped indoors during a massive New England snowstorm. The poem, dedicated "to the Memory of the Household It Describes," bears an epigraph from pseudo-Agrippa's first *Book of Occult Philosophy,* which reads: "As the Spirits of Darkness be stronger in the dark, so Good Spirits, which be Angels of Light, are augmented not only by the Divine light of the Sun, but also by our common Wood Fire: and as the Celestial Fire drives away dark spirits, so also this our Fire of Wood doth the same."

In the poem, gathered around the hearth, the Whittier family shares stories and stays safe from dark spirits strengthened in the day-destroying snowfall. Outside, "The wind that round the gables roared, / With now and then a ruder shock / ..., made our very bedsteads rock," the groaning homestead's "board-nails snapping in the frost."

In Latin, the word for "fireplace" or "hearth" or "family" is *focus*.

The iris dilates to adjust for dimness as it searches the shadows that gather in corners.

Focus.

Don't get distracted.

At the end of Whittier's poem, once the "tumultuous privacy of Storm" has passed, the speaker and his family dig themselves out of the built-up snow-banks, as though returning to the upper-world of life and light. "Wide swung again our ice-locked door, / And all the world was ours once more!" As though self-exhumed. The eye or the world as it widens.

See, I am trying to give my name to you. I am trying to do the work of decrypting what I'm telling you, as though by proxies, withdrawing from the fire's radius, coming close, but not quite, to putting it out, to desecrating by dissecting my brother's body, bringing fragments of my family life into un-light to recover something guarded jealously by angels, spirits of Celestial Fire, of this our Fire of Wood.

The bedsteads rock. The board-nails snap. Here I am, half in shadow, trying not to focus, because if I didn't keep us in the dark, nothing could be shown.

Sorry most of all that I am not sorry. I mean, I apologize I can't apologize for this. That is to say, this inability to speak, or speak directly, which is perhaps a kind of damnation already, or at least a damming, where the word "orator" or speaker has its etymology in *hretor*, so close to *hreo*, which means "to flow." To be unable to flow with speech, dammed up, full of words as one may become full of water, the perilous condition of two ancients, Socrates and Heraclitus both.

At the beginning of his *Apology*, Socrates informs his audience he is no orator, no rhetorician, unlike those who have accused him of atheism and the corruption of the Athenian youth. I am not a skillful speaker, he apologizes. His words, he promises, won't come flowingly, and the language he will speak in will be the language of the public marketplace, the place of buying and selling, even selling out.

Heraclitus, the great philosopher of paradox (literally, *to say* ["dox"] *alongside of* ["para"], or as from the corner of the mouth), died of dropsy, a disorder where the sufferer's body accumulates and retains too much water. Heraclitus, the same thinker who tells us "Into the same river twice you cannot step; other waters flow in and upon you," died dammed. In his translation of Heraclitus's fragments, the poet Dan Beachy-Quick writes of the philosopher's death:

"In many fragments, Heraclitus speaks of soul's delight in getting wet, but how that moisture is its death, that a dry soul, a soul of dry-heat, is best. Dying himself of such moisture, Heraclitus left the hills and came to town to see a doctor and ask how his intestines might be rid of the water they held. Being told there was no remedy, he plastered himself with cow dung and lay down beneath the bright sun, hoping the water would be drawn out of his body. The cure didn't work. He died at the age of sixty. Some say he was buried in the marketplace. Others that, unable to tear off the dung coating him, that dogs came and devoured him, a cynical thought where no remains remain. Just the fragments."

Unable to undam, reduced to fragments. Covered in shit. Unable to say from where I derive, or to confess the sources of my speech. Derivative from *derivare*, to "draw off a liquid," but also to "divert." Thus this ditching. These redirections and distractions.

It wasn't until our first heavy winter rain that we learned our new house was at the bottom of a gentle basin, toward which all the local surface water flowed. To avoid subsequent floods, my father dug a system of perimeter ditches, laid down preemptive sandbag barriers, and installed handmade French drains at strategic locations around our property. My brother and I were old enough to help with his efforts. At the end of every summer, before the rainy season, we would winterize by deepening the ditches, their edges eroded.

I also remember helping my father dig and lay pipe for the opposite reason: to divert water to the yard from a nearby irrigation canal, used to supply the larger vineyards, ranches, and pastures that surrounded us. My father designed his own pump and cistern and permanent sprinkler system to hold and distribute water during the hot months. Sometimes, at the end of his hydrologic labors, he would sit in a plastic chair on the back deck to drink juice and ice and watch the glittering jets of water arc across his lawn and gardens.

At these times, if I sat beside him in the shade and privacy of this dome of flying water, we could talk about anything. No subject was off-limits. Nothing was so secret or too personal. Once, for instance, as a teenager, I learned from him that my mother's health had long obstructed their sex life. At the age of twenty-seven, she had suffered a stroke that triggered chronic pain, partial paralysis, and hormonal imbalance that persists to this day. In connection with these ailments, which prevented much movement outside the narrow, uneventful radius of the home, a series of invasive, more recent surgeries had rendered certain kinds of physical intimacy almost impossible.

Without frustration or disappointment, my father implied that his own life had contracted to match hers. His energies were redirected to hobbies like bee-keeping, gardening, wood-working, home improvement, motorcycle maintenance, as well as, above all, increased focus on his church and family, builder of small kingdoms.

Growing up, I was, of course, intimately familiar with my mother's fibromyalgia. Small cuts or bruises were amplified to feel more like wounds and broken bones. She might be weeping in the kitchen, something shattered at her feet. Frequent migraines forced her to retreat in the middle of the day to her bedroom, where the noon light burned around the edges of dark blue, checkered curtains. Home electrotherapy. Cabinets filled with orange prescription bottles and jars with obscure vitamins of baroque denomination. Much of her surprising strength and resolute happiness my mother drew from her family and her faith, reading scripture and scholarly commentary every morning on the couch, before the pain and fatigue sapped her ability to focus.

Mormons believe in the eventual resurrection of the body in a perfected state, clean of blemish or disease. Though she never said so, I often wondered if my mother drew on this idea for hope.

Meanwhile, on the margins of ditches, beneath a curtain of flung water, the gardens brim with begonias, peonies, and hydrangeas, bell-flowered squash plants, massive banks of blackberries, the tiny trellising of snap-peas. A still life. There is still life.

Damnation, I was always taught in church, is a form of stoppage, a freezing of progress. Those damned are barred from the eternal growth promised in the afterlife. Here, the dam and its reservoir provide a ready metaphor.

In this light, the still life is a damned image.

Bronze hour. Broken tulips. A snail trails along a pedestal.

Abraham Mignon's seventeenth-century still life, *Flowers in a Crystal Vase, Standing on a Pedestal with a Dragonfly*: in a squat vase, a volcanic arrangement of roses, tulips, poppies, peonies, iris, orange blooms, carnation, blackberry, morning glory, bindweed, ears of wheat. Hidden among the petals, a variety of insects, including butterflies, moths, ladybugs, aphids, dragon-flies, beetles, spiders, and caterpillars. In the corner, a growing infestation of silkworms. Spun and eaten leaves. But stalled in their webbing.

According to some art historians, the plants, insects, animals, foodstuffs, and objects in a still life constitute a coded moral message. The simplest item means something, often in relation to the other objects that it's bunched with.

Ear of wheat evokes the Eucharist. Oranges and peonies stand for luxury and exotic exploration. Snail of humility, poppy of sleep. The iris, the trinity.

When I look at a still life, I try first to find a fly among the ripe and oozing grapes. Harbinger of rot. The blemishes on apple-skins or the papery copper-color of leaf-disease common to this genre have a moralizing function, a reminder of the transience of earthly life and the material world. In Mignon's painting, the caterpillars and butterflies might decode as symbols of the resurrection. But the caterpillar is as much a blight, devourer of green. The silkworms weave a shroud.

As an art form, the still life offers a tonic to history painting, to "megalography," or the depiction of grand events at an active, sweeping scale. In fact, as art historian Norman Bryson points out, "still life pitches itself at a level of material existence where nothing exceptional occurs: there is a wholesale eviction of the Event. At this level of routine existence, centred on food and eating, uniqueness of personality becomes an irrelevance. Anonymity replaces narrative's pursuit of the unique life and its adventures."

To this he adds that the "removal of the human body is the founding move of still life."

A table laid with a half-eaten meal, a hand-peeled citrus, the exhumation of a body. What we are left with is this life, the uneventful common-place, the narrowness of home and its constellation of small wares and softening fruit, randomly arranged, yet somehow also ripe with the promise of hidden meaning. Decrypt it: its moral is decryption, the resurrection and the life, a caterpillar gnawing at a leaf, damned to do so in this image of it, suspended in a niche of permanent light.

For the most I can offer you are these images, these goddamn diversions. Not events, but coded arrangements, flies and irises, strewn and tabled details of a daily life. Because, really, I have nothing special to confess: I am just like you, by which I mean I am not in this, this text, we find ourselves outside the frame, in a shared world of actual chalices, fat grapes, festering piles of smearable shit. The bodies of friends and family are not here either, having been buried and reburied, if only to make sure that they're still there, not available to you or me for use in treasure-seeking, meaning-making, the unearthing of which would only bring further hieroglyphs to light. I promise it isn't personal. I mean, when I refuse to begin by disclosing my new name, no Ishmael at the outset, inviting you to "Call me," it is not because I don't trust you, but because this could keep on going endlessly, and to withhold what would damn me, what would ex-communicate me, ensures that it does, it does go on, there is still life, the flow of writing through ditches that writing has dug, these inscriptions in the earth.

To keep ditching, but not as in to canalize or deepen. Instead, to let go, to leave be. Not to go back to the source, for once. Not to the root—of the word, of the mystery—but to the surface. Less an adventure, an adventure of the trace, than an invitation to the table, settling for what's common between us: a prayer, a shared meal. We will leave disorder when we're full and done, when our bodies have gone from the frame.

This is me, trying to remain in anonymity, at least partially, half in shadow, half out, quietly at home in what life there still is. But no, that isn't true. I have all but told you, my innermost secret more or less exposed, though there will be no total resolution, still a tugging margin of damnation, an inch or two of floodwater, a partial loss of focus.

Reduced in the end, instead, to whispers and fragments.

Trying not to do the work for you.

Encryption

In the crypt beneath Glasgow Cathedral, a patchwork quilt covers the tomb of Saint Kentigern, also known as Mungo, meaning "dear one" in a cross-stitch of Cumbric and Welsh. Bright beneath the time-dark stone, you might find a blanket just like it draped over a recliner in your grandparents' living room, folded there to keep the upholstery from tattering, from blackening with daily unguents, oil and sweat. Against a sea of gradients of blue, a patchy bonfire of orange and red engulfs a gold-embroidered latticework sewn into the quilt, an homage both to the cranes for building ships at the mouth of the nearby River Clyde and to the branch of hazel that Mungo blew into flame so as to light the chapel-lamps he was charged as a boy with keeping bright. In the weeks that followed my visit to the Cathedral, walking beside the Clyde in morning mist, I liked to picture the steel girders of the gantries in their shipyards breathed with church-fire. Or I tried to envision halves of the hull for a destroyer swinging through the air, upheld by boom and struts and groaning jib of supple limbs and twigs. In reality, the mist was only lit with vast electric billboards. For twenty seconds at a time, the nova of an Egg McMuffin blinked in and out of being on the opposite bank.

The hazel tree from which Mungo took his taper later multiplied into a quiet copse. It is rumored that nothing makes for better kindling than wood from that still-blessed grove. Dry or green, it catches easily, and spreads like thought. Ralph Waldo Emerson writes, "The true preacher can be known by this, that he deals out to the people his life—life passed through the fire of thought." The little details of a life, but wreathed in changeful flame. In the *Vita Kentigerni,* the saint's hagiographer includes a quaint description of Mungo's bed, a stone crevice that he hesitates whether to call "a bed or a tomb," a quilt or a crypt, along with a meticulous account of the saint's bathing habits. The writer invites us to consider how, when Mungo rose early to wash himself in the river, the simple act of entering the water, "naked [and] following a naked Christ," was like "entering into conflict" with Satan, that "great and malignant dragon, which, according to the prophet, lieth in the midst of his rivers." When Mungo emerged, gleaming in the stony bank-light, he was like "one of the flock that are evenshorn which came up from the washing to Mount Gilead, emerging from the water like a dove bathed in milk, yea, as a Nazarite whiter than snow, brighter than milk, ruddier than ancient ivory, fairer than a sapphire." As water runs in rivulets down his shoulders and wrists, Mungo in his whiteness morphs and shape-shifts ceaselessly, a glitching billboard in the mist. His life provides a lattice or a trellis for the discovery of correspondences and similitudes. The life of the preacher or saint is not stable as such. It is a flimsy truss of ladderwork and lessons. A spillage of sapphires, strobing liquid crystal diodes in the morning by the Clyde.

The quilt in the Cathedral shows one of four of Mungo's major miracles, images of which appear also on Glasgow's city crest. All together, the miracles are remembered in a little song or verse:

Here is the bird that never flew
Here is the tree that never grew
Here is the bell that never rang
Here is the fish that never swam

The poem reads like a riddle, or cipher, yet it withholds nothing. Quite the opposite—it renders bird, tree, bell, fish to you. Here they are—take them. But it is an odd set of clues, all the same; a list of failures, of objects and creatures that were supposed to perform a certain function, but in transgressing those functions, the inborn directives to fly, grow, ring, and swim, found a second life in miracle. It is possible to read each line as a small history of refusal. A series of infidelities, the natural course of things disrupted. The idea of a miracle that flouts ordination, that denies ecology and hierarchy may seem at first counterintuitive, even subversive. But in truth it has always been difficult to tell the difference between miracle and heresy.

Set on billboard-style struts that support electric lettering, the words "There will be no miracles here" blaze in marquee lights above the broad lawn outside the Scottish Gallery of Modern Art in Edinburgh. So positioned, it is a phrase that attended one of my first sustained experiences with contemporary art—and yet, contrary to its negative pronouncement, I left the Gallery on a warmish day in early June with a sense that reality had shifted, that nothing could be taken as given, and that everything—all the common thoroughfares and roundabouts, all the awnings and the gates and ordered hedges—were suddenly miraculous in the sense of having been placed there, arranged like art into an index of intelligence, and that intelligence ran also in the grout and masoned brick, and on the asphalt in the light between the shadows of the hazel leaves. Nathan Cooley, the artist of the installation, cites as his inspiration for the piece a proclamation by one of France's seventeenth-century kings, who made his decree in response to a sharp spike in the number of miracles reported in a southeastern village called Modseine. That there will be no miracles here is less a promise, then, than a scramble to restore right order. To foreclose on the hysteria or charlatanry that sees, for instance, in bird and bell and fish and tree not the simple things themselves, but conspiring emblems of a brighter stratum of reality.

While revising this essay, I search the internet in vain for more information on Modseine; the only hits I get are in articles about Cooley's installation. Maybe it's a made-up place, a made-up decree. The statement frantic to correct what hasn't actually been disturbed. No one risen from the dead. Trying to unsee what was never seen. Its blinding invisibility.

I recognize, of course, that my reading of Mungo's little poem is not the most obvious. Maybe it's peculiar to me. Maybe it makes more sense to say that the song is less a series of refusals—as if the bird could choose not to fly—and more a catalogue of miraculous disabilities. Each line in the poem records a miracle of damnation or preemption, of crippled estate and only partial compensation. Take the hazel tree: stripped and burned, a single tree unfolds into grove, a possible symbol of vitality and regeneration, and yet the wood therein is endowed with special flammability, a readiness to evanesce to ash. Rewarded with its own destroyability.

Or take the fish. A king learns his wife has been cheating on him with one of his young soldiers when he discovers that the queen has given her lover a ring that was originally a gift from her husband. Plotting his revenge, the king takes the soldier on a hunting trip, during which the two decide to nap for a while beside the Clyde. Instead of killing the queen's young lover as he sleeps, the king, only pretending to drowse, sneaks the ring off the other's finger and throws it into the river. On returning, the king summons the queen, confronts her with his suspicions, and demands that she produce the ring as proof of her fidelity, or else suffer execution. Learning her lover has lost it, the distraught queen sends a messenger to Mungo, begging him for help. Instead of refusing the queen on grounds of adultery, Mungo sends the messenger to the river with instruction to cut open the first fish he catches and to take the contents of the stomach to his queen. Sure enough, the messenger discovers a ring, maybe set with a sapphire, glistening in the ropy belly of a salmon. When the queen returns the precious object to her husband, the king recognizes a miracle has been performed, inspiring him to forgive his wife. And yet it is strange that the miracle is remembered today by the fish, so peripheral to the narrative, so literally disposable—for we never even learn how the messenger handled the carcass, whether he wrapped it in paper and grass to eat later, or whether he tossed the gutted body in the mud and sedge and simply hurried home. Like the hazel branch, the fish is caught up in a plot it swims a tangent to. It didn't ask to be redirected from its normal course.

So the poem can be read in at least two ways. Either the objects are errant, aberrant, unfaithful to their nature. Or they are broken, manipulated, split open, carelessly mishandled, in themselves unimportant to the larger life of the preacher or the saint who burns with thought. Or maybe they're both. Maybe their brokenness is their errancy. The fishing line a line-of-flight.

I discovered this poem when I read it printed on a postcard in the Cathedral giftshop after leaving Mungo's crypt. Doing so, I felt the city slowly shifting or grinding into place around me, self-organizing, sands in nodal lines on a resonating plate struck with the tiny hammer of that nursery rhyme. It rang true to what I thought my reason was for being there, in Glasgow, a city of no special or personal importance, in the first place. The decision to spend the summer studying in Scotland had been driven mainly by affordability and ease, and the fact that, of the programs offered by my university, it was soonest scheduled for departure. My aim was just to leave the country, to prove to myself that I could, that I wasn't somehow stuck in the States, immobilized by the experiences I had had a year before, when I had burned out as a Mormon missionary. Instead of spending two years proselyting on the streets of Paris, where I had been assigned, it had taken just three short weeks in the Missionary Training Center (or MTC) in Provo, Utah, for me to start wondering what would happen if I were to throw myself from the running track raised loft-style above a polished basketball court twenty-five or thirty feet below. I also knew that the closet near the dorm room I shared with six other nineteen-year-olds was kept unlocked and stocked with cleaning supplies, including a couple of jugs of drinkable bleach. At first, I took private pleasure in these thoughts. Along with the flimsy blades I had busted free from my disposable razor to make tiny fish-slits on my body in the bathroom stall, ideas about suicide gave me a sense of control, of final say in a life I felt I had ceded to a god I didn't believe in, and hadn't for some time, choosing to apply for service due in part to quiet pressure from friends and family, and in part to a sense of optimism that maybe I could preach the gospel at an angle, telling it but slant. Soon, though, the fantasies became more compulsive. When I wasn't learning by heart the French words for "heavenly father" or "these last or latter days," every thought would tilt to the closet or spill to the surface of the court. I guess it would have been easy enough just to leave, to walk through the main gates back into a town I knew well, where friends were, but I was filled with dread at the thought of returning eventually to a disappointed family, or to the small, rural church community in whose company I'd spent every Sunday morning in memory.

When I finally told an in-house therapist what I was thinking, and that I was cutting, it was no longer clear to me whether I confessed this because I knew they would send me home, given indefinite leave on grounds of mental health, or because I actually needed the help. Probably it was both. One imperative had dovetailed with the other, much as the image of a bather as a dove will curve into ivory, then harden as a gem, a cut stone that's hard to tell apart from the water into which it has been thrown, swallowed while it's sinking by a fish, who takes it in as nothing more substantial than a flash of light or inner ripple in the river of the body of the dragon where it swims.

Like flame, the thought gets out of hand, or burns the hand that holds it furling in a hazel branch. I let it drop. I light another one, one of anything, whatever is in reach, bird or bell, with just my breath.

Sent home, afraid that maybe I had wrecked my one chance for travel, having spent my life up to that point moving in more provincial circles, I promised myself that I would do everything I could to leave the country within a year of washing out. The destination didn't matter. I just needed to be able to feel my radius was not reduced, shrunk to fit the gridded contours of a parish. Leaving the MTC, one of the several administrators and counselors who met with me to manage my transition had glimpsed that part of me that wasn't in control and said that there were in life all types of missions. Not all of them were two years long and far from home. I can't remember if I thought about those words while standing in the giftshop tucked adjacent to the entrance to the nave, going over the slant or nonexistent rhyme of *rang* with *swam* while Mungo slept below, feeling like I'd found a coded message, a clue whose decryption would reveal to me that there was nothing random in my being here beneath this barrel vault—either that, or that randomness, with enough work, could be resolved or willed into a pattern. The poem read like evidence that my failure to become a fisher of men might have been the point. That to refuse the task that I had been raised to do was good, even a miracle in its own right.

But a miracle that manifested what? It wasn't God I felt moving in this new knowledge, or if it was a god then it was the god of movement itself, Mercury or Hermes, the god of fleet-footed messengers, of he who was sent to slit a salmon, empty it of its unwitting contents, and carry back with him a ring that could be used to pardon infidelity, faithlessness made to seem as though it never happened, a tree that never grew.

The connections, these fishing-lines-of-flight from thought to thought, aren't clear, even to me. Even to me they sound like sophistries. Like falling for false witness thoughtlessly, hook and sinker. In *Tribute to Freud*, the poet H.D. asks herself: "Do I wish myself in the deepest unconscious or subconscious layers of my being to be the founder of a new religion?" A Joseph Smith? A David Koresh? Another Anne Hutchinson, American antinomian? One cult traded for another: this time, the cult of poetry, that cult of flowing speech. One of H.D.'s first published poems, called "Hermes of the Ways," is a reimagining of an Ancient Greek epigram by Anyte of Tegea that reads in its original translation: "I, Hermes, stand here by the windy orchard in the cross-ways nigh the grey sea-shore, giving rest on the way to wearied men; and the fountain wells forth cold stainless water." H.D.'s version is written in two parts, split in half where the semi-colon shows up in the epigram, bringing with it, added almost as an afterthought, a fountain flowing at the crossroads where a three-faced god, "him / of the triple path-ways," stands in wait. In the poem's second part, the fountain wells up from under the earth and runs beneath an apple tree whose branches bear a mealy fruit, "too late ripened / by a desperate sun / that struggles through sea-mist," a mist that also fills the orchard, creating the impression that "the boughs of the trees / are twisted / by many bafflings," convolutions almost without context, almost disconnected in the sea-fog from the trunks that ground them. For a brief moment, the branches seem to the speaker like the rigging of so many ships at harbor, along the docks where hammer-head and cantilever cranes that built them also loom, lattice titans shawled at dusk in the yellow gloom of safety light, but the speaker soon concludes that "the shadow of them, / is not the shadow of the mast head / nor of the torn sails." After all, then, she has not traveled so far. She is not at sea, but still on land, surrounded by trees, in an orchard, which, as we learn from a poem that appeared alongside "Hermes of the Ways," is watched over by another, different deity— Priapus, god of fertility, of bounty and surplus. Overwhelmed by the beauty of fruit trees, so like freighters in the fog, the speaker in "Orchard" begs the orchard-god to "spare us from loveliness," the gorgeousness of what another poet, John Keats, would call a "conspir-acy" between the autumn mist and sun to "load and bless / with fruit the vines that round the thatch-eves run." No more miracles, please.

Yet, as offering to entice the god to stop, the speaker would bestow on him the very fruit that he has caused to bend the tree-boughs: her gift a cor-nucopia of "fallen hazel-nuts, / stripped late of their green sheaths, / grapes, red-purple, / their berries / dripping with wine, / pomegranates already broken, / and shrunken figs / and quinces untouched."

Maybe the idea is for gorgeousness to eat gorgeousness, and, glutted, fall asleep and give us peace.

But the poem doesn't say anything about whether the offering will do the trick. Its logic leaves us only with an ouroboros, growth annihilating growth. A self-dismantling with the self's own produce. A self-interment that secures that self. A burial in life that, the poet Rainer Maria Rilke reminds, will bring forth that life again—although "invisibly," as though in an overblessed but nonexistent province conjured as a pretext for the billboard burning on the green.

For Rilke, the deeper the burial, the more assured this exhumation: "It is our task to imprint this provisional, perishable earth so deeply, so pa-tiently and passionately in ourselves," he writes, "that its reality shall arise in us again 'invisibly.' We are the bees of the invisible." Such is the poet's work. Reality shall rise again, but first it has to die in me. I have to encrypt it. Or, rather, I have to decrypt it—that is, make a slit from its anus to its neck, killing it, but for good reason.

Or, by Rilke's thinking: in encrypting, I decrypt.

Left, anyway, to my own devices, a word that could mean heraldry, a sign on a crest or on a coat-of-arms wrought into a shield that I picked up at random, the readiest defense. Glasgow's city seal has as its device a dense knot of images: a bird in a tree hung with a bell, at the base of which is an upturned fish with a ring in its mouth. It's a riddle; solve it: each object stands for a damning, the result of which was miracle, the bringing-forth of something true—an un-secreting or flourishing, the growth of an invisible flower.

You can't see them, so you'll have to trust me that they're there. Try to picture on this shield, this blank page between us, a far field of them, of apple trees in bloom but sheathed in mist, and rioting beneath the darkened orchard's spreading canopy a faintest tracery of tulips and poppies, of peonies and carnations, imprint of ivy and roses in invisible ink:

Fire or Lime

Ivy, roses, songbirds. What types, I don't know. Nor am I certain, for that matter, that I'm looking at roses or ivy at all in the patterned screen-print of the shower-curtain in my grandmother's guest bathroom. It might be safer to say leaves and flowers and songbirds—or even just plain birds. For song is an assumption, too. Sometimes it's safer to surrender one kind of accuracy. Otherwise, you risk admitting what was never there.

The curtain is embossed as well as screen-printed: under the visible layer, there are outlines of other types of foliage. I expect to find an echo of the same ivy-rose design, but instead the ghostly flora there looks nothing like the rose, nor the ivy-leaf. The encrypted flowers are big, ruffly, tropical. The leaves are like oak. Or perhaps maple. There are no birds.

For as long as I can remember, my grandparents have lived among the oaks and madrones in Scotts Valley, California. Before it was incorporated, the area was home for several years to Sky Park Airfield, a small municipal airport. Today, the airstrip asphalt is barely traceable under the crab-grass of the vacant lot north of the city's actual park. The mural on the nearby public library shows a yellow Beechcraft dragging a banner that says, *"Remembering Sky Park Airport 1947 to 1983."* It is a few days after Christmas, which means school is still on holiday, and kids are in the park and in the empty lot, which is made up of gravel, old asphalt, and mud turned up by tire-tread. A father and son troubleshoot a balsa wood airplane powered by a rubber-band.

During its lifespan, short on space for take-off and landing, Sky Park struggled for grants and government support: the original runway wasn't angled right. Steve Wozniak, the co-founder of Apple, crashed his private plane here in 1981, suffering some facial scarring, as well as temporary short-term memory loss.

The idea is to go later to the lime kilns in Felton. The whole West rests on the back of the lime kiln, its gold boom-towns made from mortar made from baked-down stone. My grandmother had trouble this Christmas with her mom's white layer-cake recipe. It crumbled like it was too fresh, she says. Impossible to keep up the architecture of layered cake and cream. She had to settle for a kind of trifle. My dad points out that it sounds like a problem with the oil or eggs. She admits to using large eggs and substituting olive oil when she should have put in vegetable, acknowledging the risks of using whatever was on hand.

The blue of the sweat-suit my grandmother wears to hike the kilns in Henry Cowell Redwoods State Park is the same blue as the knitted baby shoes my father wore, a newborn, fifty-five years ago. She hands the shoes down to my mother. The hope is to return these things to life. Before she recovered them digging through deep storage, there was nobody to know or recall they existed, these mementos of the mothering she'd done.

The trail is a little over a mile in length. My grandmother, who had not anticipated the hard terrain, brings along the dog stroller to lean on. My dad and brother have to lift it, with her terrier inside, over roots, runoff, stones. The mind has a hard time adjusting. The bathroom feels a little farther every night.

At the turn of the twentieth century, Henry Cowell, one of the lime barons of Santa Cruz County, competed with the city and the H.T. Holmes and the I.X.L. companies for acreage forested with enough redwood to fuel a demand for lime in San Francisco and Santa Cruz proper. It took three to four days and seventy cords of timber gorged from the surrounding forest to burn off the carbon and leave behind a thousand pounds of calcium oxide, also known as lime. Lime was used for mortar to build cities and later rebuild them when they crumbled and burned on top of fault-lines. What redwoods are left have been consecrated a state park and have taken Cowell's name.

Highway 9 bullwhips through the Park, which you can't avoid if you want to get to the beach or boardwalk from Felton. Everywhere there seems to be a park entrance or pull-off for easy access. My dad worked his college summers clearing trail and building bridges over Fall and Bennett creeks for the Forest Service. On these my grandmother and grandfather now struggle for their footing. At first, they will hear nothing about turning back. As a consequence, later, at night, from the guest room, I can hear in their bedroom the chuff of my grandfather's hands on my grandmother's feet and legs as she moans from pain, only now setting in.

Eventually, we start to separate. My brother and I go on ahead through the dense green foliage of the woods to scout the way and see how much of the one and two-tenths of a mile remain until the kilns. Soon after we peel off, my mom and dad and sister follow. My grandparents have decided to turn back after all, and they make good time. For a while, the family is stretched in a line through the woods, taut string in a chord.

Shoulderless, the frontage road from Santa Cruz to Scotts Valley carves under Highway 17, hollows out an overpass. To get the concrete beams for this span of bridge to set, the CDOT must have used wooden panels to keep it all in place, since the cement there is impressed with knots and grain from lengths of pine supports.

My grandfather's father was a carpenter, too. In the dusk, I help my dad move a heavy table saw from the shop underneath his parents' mobile home into the truck-bed. On a workbench in the shop are stencils and wood rounds painted with Pennsylvania Dutch hex signs. The mighty oak's mystery: strength, health in body and mind, long life. A scalloped border is the sea, smooth sailing it. My grandfather's father, also a Harold, took to sea fishing, especially salmon, and was in the Vancouver *Sun* once for landing a forty-pound chinook with his brother, Cyril. The columnist admits the actual weight of the fish was 39 ¾ pounds, but says that "if it had eaten a couple more herring before it inhaled Cyril's it would have been a 40."

The *Sun* clippings have floated to the floor from a binder that holds, in a transparent sleeve, the pocket-sized version of the *Book of Psalms* that belonged once to Harold Sr. A gift, it bears the inscription: "From Cyril Rice 552-21st st Brandon Man To his Brother Private H. Rice God Watch over you + Bring you safe back When you pray say our Father." I use my new iPhone, a Christmas present, to photograph this blessing and exhortation.

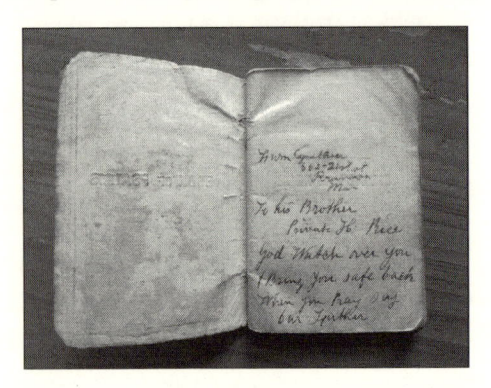

After a married couple from Redlands shot and killed fourteen people in San Bernardino, the FBI appealed to Apple, Inc. to make software to give them backdoor access to the encrypted contents of one of the terrorists' iPhones. Apple refused, and the FBI found a third-party work-around. A few months later, during a Reddit AMA, Steve Wozniak addressed the subject of Apple's security policies, reflecting more broadly on his philosophy of privacy:

"…You know what, I have things in my head, some very special people in my life that I don't talk about, that mean so much to me from the past. Those little things that I keep in my head are my little secrets. It's a part of my important world, my whole essence of my being. I also believe in honesty. If you tell somebody, 'I am not snooping on you,' or, 'I am giving you some level of privacy; I will not look in your drawers,' then you should keep your word and be honest. And I always try to avoid being a snoop myself, and it's rare in time that we can look back and say, 'How should humans be treated?' Not, 'How can the police run everything?'

"…So, I come from the side of personal liberties. But there are also other problems. Twice in my life I wrote things that could have been viruses. I threw away every bit of source code. I just got a chill inside. These are dangerous, dangerous things, and if some code gets written in an Apple product that lets people in, bad people are going to find their way to it, very likely."

How slippery some lines of code. How indiscernibly a back-door appears. How easy it is to open once it does.

Best not to think to write it in in the first place. There are no drawers here. There isn't even a room for an armoire to be in. Whether there are paintings hanging on the wall in this room for which there is no entrance is an immaterial concern. As soon as there is something on the page, it may be too late. The problem with writing anything is what it might admit.

For Christmas, my grandfather gives me a Dover paperback with a selection of poetry written during World War I. I open it up to Wilfred Owen's poem "Dulce Et Decorum Est," which I once had memorized for a competition in high school, and read out some lines to the gathered family:

"But someone still was yelling out and stumbling / and floud'ring like a man in fire or lime."

Calcium oxide, it turns out, is as good for building cities as for breaking down dead matter, decomposing bodies in the bottoms of trenches. The etymology for "lime"—a word also used to refer to birdlime, a sticky substance spackled onto tree-branches in order to capture perching birds—traces back to Middle and Old English terms meaning both "limb" and "mud." Materials as good for building words as muddying them together, a paste for trapping birds, which flounder on the limbs they land on.

When I ask my grandfather about his interest in World War I, he tells me his father served in the Canadian Expeditionary Forces, 181st Battalion, Brandon, Manitoba, and shows me a picture of Platoon 2. When I ask him if his father ever spoke about the war, he has a hard time remembering. This is more and more the case. He tells me instead about the Shaughnessy Military Hospital in Vancouver. He remembers using the elevator. He remembers seeing a soldier on a gurney. He remembers it was a good, long, and rare conversation with his dad, who died in the night, aged seventy-seven, cancer of the throat.

This gift is meant as a kind of fine, complicating knot. An imperfect joinery. Poetry for me, his father for him. My grandmother says she, too, loved my grandfather's father, and tells a story: Once, when my own father was young, no older than six months, the whole family went out for a fishing trip. When my dad's older sister wasn't looking, Harold Senior put a fish on her hook and slipped it back in the shallows. The illusion was real enough to thrill a three-year-old, who looked to the end of her line, and pulled, and saw her wildest imaginings rewarded. A glistening rainbow the length of her arm.

Here is a fish that never swam. A miracle, materialized. As if out of thin air: a trick out of love.

The kilns comprise a ruined stone slot in a hillside. A manufactory, now cryptic. All told, little is left. There isn't much to see. Maybe that's for the best. For the danger is that I will—by accident, erring—see what wasn't meant for me. Say what isn't there. I'll go too far and write by accident a backdoor where there should be none. For there is no house here. No grave either. And I am digging from the thin air no actual bodies.

Emerson knew the risks of synthesis. He knew that some parts of the world are better left imperfectly joined. Some connections left unmade, unmanufactured. He describes the dangers of the aging mind, which fuses into one what should be many:

> "To the young mind, every thing is individual, stands by itself. By and by, it finds how to join two things, and see in them one nature; then three, then three thousand; and so, tyrannized over by its own unifying instinct, it goes on tying things together, diminishing anomalies, discovering roots running under ground, whereby contrary and remote things cohere, and flower out from one stem."

What kind of flower is it, I wonder. Perhaps a rose, I think, or something more toxic—a bandolier of foxglove. But, to be honest, I couldn't tell you. It's safer that way. I mean, the memory, with its three thousand glistening scales, innocent of the hand that wrote it there. There, at the end of the line, where any thing could be.

E

But what good is an invisible flower?

The idealist would answer me: Your thinking is all wrong. The flower is not what's invisible, but what underlies it. What makes it possible—it, and the world. But wait. I mean it when I say the world is possible, and only that. What you see—the visible, true flower—is only a pregnancy, a heralding, an expression of potentials in a world that is potential, all: that is, one that never fully flowers, or does, but halfway: in the form of a flower. The kind that you see.

The idealist would tell me: and that flower you see—by seeing it, it's seed in you. It's not that that flower is, as such, actually in you. Instead, seen into seed, it becomes possible in you, something both more and less than what it is in truth, an eidos or idea, image that splits its bran and ramifies into the dark, and also toward the light.

Remember Rilke: *Reality shall arise in us again.*

But it's hard for me to actually believe that. Not when, in reality, there's nothing underlying anything—just surfaces, overlays, grounds that grind across each other, subducting like plates, molten again, then hardening to rise, more buoyant than the rest. Then clay, then dirt. And then, one billion years later, a super bloom flares across the valleys that the interstate transects. But, take care—this massive flowering will last for only a handful of days, then wither in the heat, then unmanage into flammability.

But the breast is no such soil—that's just an analogy. I can't take anything to heart. Or maybe, if I'm being truthful, what I mean is that I don't. I refuse to. For it's a cruel month when the snow subsides, and reality rises, green and longing and rupturing through.

In case of crisis, the United States government stores billions of seeds at the seed bank on the Colorado State University campus. Some seeds, the oldest ones—ancient strains of rice, say—are subdued by subzero temperatures in cryogenic chambers. Other more stable seeds are kept in cold storage, at warmer, yet still freezing, temperatures. These are ordered into searchable white packets and indexed on shelves, as in a library.

I tour the seed bank as part of a two-day seminar, attended by poets, animal scientists, risk managers, and also potters and installation artists from around the country. The seminar, a focus group on "Crisis and Creativity," is led by my teacher, D, a poet. The participants are his friends and students. The governing question for us is: to what extent does crisis inform creativity? Or perhaps, what does creativity look like in crisis?

During one session, the group is led in guided meditation by another poet, who instructs me and all of us to remember a childhood room. She tells me to think of that room, and all the objects in it. Now, leave it. As you leave, look to your right. Though you can't see it, though there is no door, know that, in this, your oldest, dearest home, there is a secret room beside the room in which you spent your youth. It is a room you will never enter. It is a room hung within with pictures you will never see.

Now, leave it alone. Now, leave your home.

That room I didn't know was there still grits like a spore in me.

Or, it's like an urn to me. The kind in his "Ode" that Keats held, and agonized over, and could not open up, nor ever see inside.

During another session, we meet in the ceramics studio on campus, where a potter provides the group with clay and some suggestions for touching it. We pass a warm spring afternoon in quiet labor, building up, then ruining, our small, still-pliant structures.

I decide to make a tiny urn. I decide I will give it no base, so that it has two mouths, open at both ends. The open base will be able to hide a portable speaker, which will allow me to play sounds through it, turning the urn into a speaking thing. The sounds I decide to play through it are recordings I have made of robins in song. I have manipulated the recording so that, intermittently, a fragment of a lecture by the poet and translator Anne Carson interrupts the robins in their chorus. In her sing-song shard, Carson recites a Greek nonsense word used in grieving:

otototoi popoi

On the surface of the urn, I inscribe in Greek what is inscribed on the forecourt at the Temple of Delphi:

γνῶθι σεαυτόν
Know thyself.

All in all, the work is not well-wrought. But it plants its seed in me: the next winter, I decide to take a pottery course, and I start throwing cups and bowls for real.

It's a winter of heavy snow. But the winter kept us warm, T and me, as though beneath a quilt, pretending to make a house within a house of blankets and sheets while watching our friends' kids. In that house, too, there is a hidden room. And in the rooms that winter makes we met, in the knee-deepest sense, and spoke of poetry, and pottery, for her brothers both were potters, and she herself so drawn to the vessel-form, the eidos of it, as a seed is to the lip of a seedleap, sown. And as I worked on pots, we both worked on poems for each other, using them as tools or vessels to say back to each other the things we might have said the night before, as we lay on her bed and watched the ceiling flicker with candle-light and shadows from a vase filled with winter twigs.

When the deep snows were pushed aside at last, so was the quilt.

As if for no other reason than a changed wind: the first warm night of the year, at dinner together, we fell to talking about her ex-husband, who one night hurled a kitchen-knife at her head. The sheer dead lift it took to get out from under him. Then, on her own at last, the clove cigarettes she took to smoking with the window open in the middle of winter, the midnights surging through in a dry cold wash, an underground river.

Re-opening that window in spring, peonies appear on the table and also open. She turns away from me, feeling, instead of me, a chill on her cheek.

Works by the Danish ceramicist Axel Salto have been described as organic, volcanic, demonic.

Salto's vases develop across three distinct stages. These three types are his "fluted," "budding," and "sprouting" forms. His surfaces are in process, becoming. They undergo seed and pod-like deformations into inscrutable, unspeakable plants. They do not burst, but bulge. Salto writes, "It is of greater importance for an artist to create in the spirit of nature, rather than to imitate its exterior." To make a form that channels forming. A demon is that which manifests itself from a realm of unfathomable concealment.

My pottery teacher tasks me to reproduce one of Salto's most demonic vases, the "Core of Power." My job is to channel a channeling. I fire it three times, glaze and reglaze. Foregrounds recede, the surface starts to speak, or shriek. When I finish, I call it "Grecian Urn," after Keats.

The firing process all but obliterates my original surface, a relief molded to look like a trellis in a vineyard, but turned upside down, so that the branches become roots that seem to feed upward into the volcanic, arched triple-fate of flutes.

On the surface of the vase, the vineyard becomes an inverted world, subterranean, a tunnel system for a liquid earth. In the *Inferno,* Dante and Virgil must climb down the hairy leg of Satan, who is buried to his waist at the lowest point of the universe. Once they reach and cross the threshold of that lowermost point, clinging to Lucifer's infernal body, the world rights itself, and Dante finds himself hanging upside down in purgatory.

On cold nights after working, I would exit the studio, and breathe in, and taste the clay dust trapped in the chambers of my lungs. The urn in me. Hard to handle, much less look inside. In his "Ode to a Grecian Urn," Keats has similar trouble breathing, holding a vase with a cameo that shows a classic scene that's stopped in time, "all breathing human passions far above." Keats, with "a burning forehead, and a parching tongue," pants to know what the urn contains, or what it signifies, thinking that the knowledge may be enough to quench some greater thirst. It isn't clear what stops the poet from bringing the urn to his lips and tipping it back. Perhaps the surface, stopped in time, communicates its freeze. Or maybe he intuits the consequences that come of quenching thirst, as envisioned in one of Keats's fragmentary epics, "The Fall of Hyperion, A Dream." As the poem opens, its speaker stumbles across the abandoned remnants of a feast, but still with plenty of good things left to eat and drink. Surfeiting himself on summer fruits, the wanderer gets thirsty, and sees near at hand "a cool vessel of transparent juice / Sipp'd by the wander'd bee." But the draught proves perilous: it sucks him down into a life-draining sleep, and when he wakes, he finds that he has been transported to a vast stone temple, sprawled among a heap of robes, golden tongs, censers, chafing dishes, girdles, chains, and holy jewelries thrown together at the bottom of a flight of steps that the poet begins to climb with mortal difficulty. On summiting, he discovers a dwindling fire of leaves and spice-wood, tended by a single shrouded priestess who tells him he has been permitted to dream of this temple, to "usurp this height," because he is one to whom "the miseries of the world / are misery." Surely, the poet exclaims, there are others also stung by empathy, by all the worldly sorrows, and yet—yet this temple is empty but for me. To which the priestess responds:

"'They whom thou spak'st of are no visionaries,'
...'They are no dreamers weak,
They seek no wonder but the human face;
No music but a happy-noted voice—
They come not here, they have no thought to come—
And thou art here, for thou art less than they—
What benefit canst thou do, or all thy tribe,
To the great world? Thou art a dreaming thing,
A fever of thyself. Think of the Earth;
What bliss even in hope is there for thee?...'"

In his own dream, the dreamer is damned for dreaming, for being blind to the human face, but is at least given access to this stone temple and its burning altar, where some remains of an offering no longer smolder. Here the poet cannot worship, though he wishes he could. In answer to his wishful look, the priestess cries:

"'The sacrifice is done, but not the less
Will I be kind to thee for thy goodwill.
My power, which to me is still a curse,
Shall be to thee a wonder; for the scenes
Still swooning vivid through my globed brain,
With an electral changing misery,
Thou shalt with those dull mortal eyes behold,
Free from all pain, if wonder pain thee not...'"

Thus, in a dense forest in a deep dream inside a domed, doomed temple strewn with strange vessels, the dreaming poet descends to a deeper depth, actually passing through the priestess's veiled and cryptic face as if entering a room wherein he sees things that he can't unsee, for nor can she. There, a fever of himself, he witnesses a scene of fallen gods with realmless eyes. And the gods say: "Moan. Moan, moan, moan, moan." And if the urn could speak, maybe that's what it would say. Or it might say what stone temples do:

γνῶθι σεαυτόν

According to Plutarch, in addition to this ancient scrap of wisdom ("know thyself"), there was also etched into the forecourt at Delphi a large letter E, the fifth letter of the Greek alphabet. Nobody knows what it means, least of all Plutarch, though he did try to decipher its significance:
The sun is the second planet, and E the second vowel.
Or, E means "if." As in the prayer, "if only."
Or, as in the logical syllogism: "If-then."
Or, E, the second-person singular of the verb "to be," when used to address the sun-god Apollo: "Thou art."
To say, "If only sun was and you were, too."
To say what the urn says, and by polysemy, a word that seeds and seeds and seeds.

Concrete

At first in flickering gaps, then in a break in the trees along the freeway, I catch a glimpse of another cluster of concrete columns, a complex temple of belts, of pipelines. It shutters back into the dense woods. Then the view flares open again, and we're over a big body of water on what used to be a steel through-truss double-deck, now a super-stretch of fresh concrete fixed in the sky on pylons.

I peel my eyes for mile markers, exit signs, so that later on I can route back here on Google Maps and flesh out this glimpse of a grain elevator. What I saw turns out not to be for grain at all. The silo cells belong to the Redding, California extension of the Lehigh Southwest Cement Company, based out of Texas. Outside their parking lot, there's a free-standing bas-relief frieze with two figures—one bare-headed, clutching a gear to his chest, the other casqued in a centurion's helmet, holding a lamp aloft. The frieze bears an inscription: "Safety Follows Wisdom."

Back in Colorado, my friend's Honda Civic takes the turn too quick into his girlfriend's cul-de-sac, spins out on ice, and we get to watch the world tilt—Sunday ferris-wheelers—as the car grinds to a halt on its own weight. His is a PhD in O Chem, but he wishes more he had a Jeep, a real "man-Jeep," stripped of all its extras, so he can go around winching people out of snow drifts, then send them on their way. Do the world some real—a more concrete—good.

Closer to the city center, snow plows are more thorough sowing gravel to keep tires from sliding. It, too, is mined from someplace, processed, strewn from open hoppers for safety and tread.

You don't know it, since they are filled up with water and made into lakes, but the fenced-off swatches of blue calm out by Butterfly Woods were good grounds once for gravel-mines. Seven degrees out, I walk the five miles to Martin Marietta Materials, which digs up aggregates from pits. Under cover of ice and snow, the fake lakes have become vast and unexplored clearings. Big voids barred by chain link.

What filled them once is bedrock now for asphalt draped over it like a hot broadcloth. The road beneath you hums—every now and then a knock below the chassis, indicating a seam or a suture—as people get where they're going, or even just going, for going is plenty.

To secure structural integrity for a grain elevator—unadorned, corrugated, slip-formed from concrete—a builder should figure out and account for the cool, shifting coefficient of grain weight, as well as the coefficient of friction during loading and offload. You risk trauma during voiding, trauma being filled. Cracks on the one hand, spontaneous combustion on the other.

Look on my works, says the inscription on his pedestal, Ozymandias half-in and half-out of the lone, level, semi-fluid sand, the irony of his shattered face somewhere nearby. When the poet Percy Bysshe Shelley wrote his "Ozymandias," inspired by newspaper accounts of the Italian explorer Giovanni Battista Belzoni's excavation and transport of the massive seven-and-a-quarter ton bust of Rameses II in 1817, the poet had never seen (and never would see) nor ever read descriptions of the visage he described as sneering, commanding, frowning with "wrinkled lip." In fact, far less expressive, the giant graven image of Rameses (whose Greek name was Ozymandias) looks more like the Sphinx, cryptic yet placid. The poet's mediated vision blind to the obscurer reality, to the smiling cipher behind the works of his we are commanded to look on and despair, though those works aren't there. All that remains is the maker's sunken face, wrought by someone else's hand.

With your own face sunken in the hard but shifting beads of stored wheat, you become conscious now of nostril, now the hollow where the eye is. The feeling recalls the pleasures of the metal pin-toy that you can use to make an imprint of your palm, or a 3D relief of your face, the cool manyness of all the little rods against your cheek, your forehead, shifting to account for your features as you press it there. Plunging yourself in total darkness, hoping to render yourself your own image. The product is the approximation an impression is. Mouth open, pins irony against the tongue, grotesque comic death-mask formed from out of a receptive shallowness.

In the semi-fluid, of sand, of berries of wheat, I look for my own face. I look for my own face.

In the grain elevator, which rises sphinxlike over the plains and the canebrake, I look for a symbol, some way to scrutinize this great barrier reef of concrete cylinders, no telling what's holed up inside. What good.

Rice, soybean, sunflower seeds. Or perhaps it stores up concrete itself. Powdered concrete kept in concrete, stuff of walls, eminent as it is at keeping out the wet.

I keep running aground of these. These sound vacuums.

As they spread west, Americans drifted from the square European warehouses, better suited for stacked burlap, toward the silo-form, since more and more they were dealing in bulk transport, in the beds of hopper cars and trucks. Early infrastructure of shipping and receiving in the big void inlands. Goods in diastole, then in systole as well.

I am able to feel my own heartbeat deflected back to me, in this pressure I exert on my face, trying to look on my works, to see what concrete good they do.

In cells attached to a headhouse, the silo body gets slip-form poured, new installments of concrete added once every six hours, welling the gap between two yoked wood rings. As soon as the mixture sets, the rings can be raised on screw jacks, making room for a new pour. A block of continuous, unribbed pillars can be erected this way in a handful of days.

Continuous concrete and rebar, veiling access to what's behind it.

For the minds behind the first slip-form silo, the question was: how do you make a monolith. One whole thing without segments, seams, sectors of weakness. How do you absorb a vector of pressure. The mute weight of a good.

In addition to these blocks of solid hollows, the grain elevator has for headdress an apparatus of routing pipes and wire rigging. The visual effect is naval. Warships with sails furled. Just outside Ault, Colorado, destroyers weigh anchor beside the railroads, a prairie-version of the Hudson River Defense Reserve. In 1953, the Reserve was repurposed as a flotilla of water-borne silos: someplace for the US government to store the 53 million bushels of surplus subsidized wheat it was obliged to buy from its own farmers, and now had to let rot in the holds and hulls of a peacetime fleet.

The question was: how do you shore up an economy of family farms.

I keep trying to wash up on that shore, that land. I keep hurling myself overboard, hurtling down Highway 287. But even out here, landlocked, I find myself landless. The rocks themselves are adrift, wandering Planctae,

Symplegades. A froth of men in their lee. A shattered shipping route.

Not far from the grain elevators of the Eastern Plains, the university hosts an unprepossessing seed bank in a blank building beside a railway that cuts the college town in two. Half a million seed packets in a cold storage vault laid out in shelves—much like a library. Eleven strains of wild rice preserved for progeny in cryogenic vats. A polysemy. Meaning many seeds, meaning many meanings. They run through the hand, colder than clear water.

It could be soybean. It could be corn, or wheat. Hard red, soft white. It could be rice. It could be sugar beet. It could be birdseed, or sun-cured alfalfa. It could be aggregates, gravel. It could be concrete. It could be sub-atoms, on the precipice of fusion or fission, stored in silos repurposed for missiles.

Reality, my friend J tells me as we take a regional bus down to Boulder, is what imposes itself on us. He cites Charles Sanders Peirce. He points to a metal handrail. Just so, a person is no less real than this. Yes, a person can be less real to me than this, depending on how they press and weigh on me.

As he speaks, through the winter and street salt smear on the window-glass, a landscape floats by, barns and silos above his head, goats and brides in a dream-like Chagall.

This land was made (for you and me)

There are two ways you know you are nearing, or in, or passing through Wamsutter, Wyoming. One is the bulb-shaped water tower with the town's name painted on it, which stands beside a cell-site on an unpaved street called Pipeline Road. The other is the big Love's truck stop and fill-up station, complete with an eatery and a Janus-faced menu marquee: half Subway, half fried-chicken franchise. Love's is the commercial hub of an oil town made up mostly of structures that can be hitched and hauled away.

Wamsutter is the midpoint between Salt Lake City and Fort Collins, a seven-and-a-half-hour trip. When I move from Utah to Colorado (and every time since I've shuttled in between), I stop at Love's for a tank of gas and a lunch and a leak.

That first time, I saw a want-ad posted above the urinal listing a variety of open positions at the Wamsutter location, including cashier, lube mechanic. Three years pass and I still wonder about the possibilities presented by that ad. I wonder what it might be like to vanish into the woodwork—into the flat, snow-fenced corridors of southern Wyoming, a place where fitting in is a function of taking on a gently-undulating, scrub-weed sameness.

If ever I describe this day-dream to my friends, I also outline the lengths I imagine I would have to go to in preparation. To blend in, I speculate, I would have to put on weight, bulk up, cut off my hair, turn toward silence, since otherwise my language would betray me, which is to say it would break the illusion. In this dream, dream of receding-in, I think what I am looking for is anonymity, a still life, but even as I say it, I know that the possibility of these easy morphologies against the backdrop of a landscape not actually empty is only available to me because I am white and passably masculine. Beneath the basic plains, fractured for fuel, a Byzantine geology of blood and gold. And the simple surface life a life of privilege, and a pipe dream, too, since work, in reality, never made a life simple.

Regardless of my measures, my friend H tells me, you would never fit in in such vernacular parts.

These here parts.

For the parts aren't yours.

Fragments of different species of wood, wedged together just so, create a figure, a picture, an illusion of depth. Depth in the different grains, darks and reds. An image emerges from the imperfect joinery. Now an old man, my grandfather, a long-time amateur carpenter, has turned to intarsia, the word for this method of woodwork, and set about scroll-sawing fasciae to adorn his home and ours. For ours, a wooden Winnie the Pooh. For his, an apple, its leaf, a grinning worm emerging.

Worm that makes of apple flesh all one corridor. Worm that could bore to the surface as if from out of nowhere. Out of anywhere, I mean.

In the town I live in, you drive east and cross rail six or seven times. There is not just one cut, no one easy bisection, no one side West.

It intersects whichever road at a different angle each time. A train can appear from nowhere. In the morning, in the middle of the night, squalling now through the center of town, now along its outermost edge. Most days the big BNSF engines haul hopper cars and oil tanks, or—some two or three days out of the year—white wind turbines, leviathans, lying beached, each on its own flat-bed. Other times, you stumble across a train-yard, and there is an endless mile of empty pallet-cars, stalled there for the winter.

In *Moby-Dick*, a book about obsessions, yes, but also, obsessively, about oil and its extraction, Herman Melville writes about whales in much the same way as these cars that could be anywhere: "Some whales have been captured far north in the Pacific, in whose bodies have been found the barbs of harpoons darted in the Greenland seas." Ishmael claims the "realities of the whaleman" are the realities in which wrecks of sea-going ships float up from the bottoms of lakes in the peaks of Portuguese mountains. Realities in which the fountains of Syracuse in Sicily are fed by underground rivers, whose waters tunnel all the way back to the Holy Land. For the sea and for the whale, this world is all one corridor, above which drift the continental plates, arranged in imperfect joinery.

As of the world as in it. Into its woodwork.

As we drive the rigid grid of unpaved roads of the Pawnee grasslands, roads rock-hardened by mag chloride sprayed from time to time to tamp down dust, my friend M and I pass tanker trucks and flat-beds hauling things for drilling. All morning we see only one other passenger car, a pick-up truck, three men in it. One waves. M returns the wave and reckons them oilmen. Everyone is an oilman out here, one way or another. One way or another, you get tangled in the infrastructure, and in the endless empty miles in between.

A buzz-cut, more muscle, the day's drive it takes to get to anywhere. Far away, a part. So a part there is no extracting. No fracturing, hydraulic or otherwise. So engrained in an economy there is no other use for me. No possible repurposing. No fathoming any other outcome.

Free will, a thread headed by the needle of chance, gets interwoven with the warp of necessity. It is thus that Ishmael extrapolates from the weave of a mat the workings of the world.

At the Twin Pillars of the Pawnee Buttes, aberrant humps of land breach the prairie sea. We stand at the trailhead and look at the vista and state park signage. M and I have taken the morning to visit the birth-site of the horse. It is reckoned so by a sign posted on the front door of the High Plains Historical Society's Museum in Nunn, Colorado, which says: "We believe the horse developed first here in North America. He grew over the centuries 50 miles north east of Nunn at a sight known as the twin pillars of the Pawnee Buttes. Also a Folsom arrow point was found in the same area."

Here, apparently, in America First, the horse species developed its fitness, its fittedness. Back when Bering was a bridge and less a strait. When East was not cloven from West, and the Clovis, pre-Folsom, came across.

An informational passage on the sign at the trailhead for the Twin Pillars invites its readers to consider the strong wind assailing them. So much a fixture it warrants an inscription. The wind as if written in stone. I can almost imagine these buttes more wind-formed than worn down by some long-gone sea.

But it is the sea that has made the world a corridor. A hallway. A hallway of rooms, none of which conclude in themselves. Each room an anteroom. The Holy Land an anteroom to Syracuse, New York. This is the reality of the whaleman.

Whalemen were oilmen, too. Melville reminds his reader that the lamps of the world—"all the tapers, lamps, and candles that burn round the globe"—burn with light that feeds on oil, oil from the whale, its fatty parts.

In the shadows that swarm at the edges of the taper-glow you read this by: a swarm of swallowed krill.

Entangled in the whale-lines of geocapital and industry, the world is all one passage. Passing through Pawnee, a wave exchanged.

For the working person, the person being worked out, everything returns to that work. That working of the world. That working in. He becomes so invested in forces larger than him, larger than life, that it becomes impossible to tell himself apart. It becomes impossible to say, *here is where I start.* It becomes impossible to say. Everything is just so. Just so, on the Pequod, the working oilmen "were one man, not thirty. For as the one ship that held them all; though it was put together of all contrasting things— oak, and maple, and pine wood; iron, and pitch, and hemp—yet all these ran into each other in the one concrete hull, which shot on its way, both balanced and directed by the long central keel; even so, all the individualities of the crew, this man's valor, that man's fear; guilt and guiltiness, all varieties were welded into oneness, and were all directed to that fatal goal which Ahab their one lord and keel did point to."

On Holocaust Remembrance Day, Donald Trump signs a presidential order barring entrance to refugees immigrating from countries with terrorist concerns. America first. An "American carnage" is how Trump describes the state of the nation's extractive industries and infrastructure.

A Jewish art dealer named Adolph Loewi immigrated from Italy to America in the summer of 1939 to escape Nazi persecution. Loewi's was, until his expatriation, a successful, well-regarded firm. Much of his stock of paintings, sculpture, and decorative arts like textiles and costumes Loewi had to leave behind in Italy, but he instructed specially that the wood intarsia paneling of the Studiolo Gubbio be shipped overseas to him. Eventually, needing cash, he sold the work to the Metropolitan Museum for thirty-thousand dollars, having first asked double that.

Once the walls for a room in the ducal palace at Gubbio, in Italy, the panels, inlaid with several different types of wood, trick the eye into seeing depth where it isn't. There are cupboards filled with objects like books and swords. There are porphyry roundels. There are long shadows cast, as if the room within a room has been stalled in time, fixed at some late hour of the day, sunlight worked in in wood at a golden angle.

Oak, maple, pine.

Hemp, iron, pitch.

Curators at the Met sent measurers to Gubbio to get the original dimensions of the study, and have used them to reproduce, as others have before, this wandering room. This time on 5th Avenue, in New York City, a few blocks up from Trump Tower. The illusion works because its vanishing points are built-in, are part of the infrastructure. A total environment, every time the room has been dismantled, shipped by rail or boat, it's taken with it—the clothes on its back—its own recession into its own distance. Which is not distance, but woodwork. Not far away, but parts. An imperfect joinery from all over of oak, maple, pine.

A synthesis becomes the distance I vanish into, the illusion of fitness fulfilled.

That's the dream anyway. If not myself to wander, tectonic, all slippage and subduction, then to recognize the world as it wanders underneath me, uneasily. The real dream to recognize that I am dreaming and return to the real, which is to say the concrete world, what Emerson, the American sage, describes as one of surfaces only, among which the "true art of life" is to learn "to skate well on them." Yet these surfaces suggest a depth. And yet that depth is an effect of woodwork, fragments of walnut, beech, rosewood, oak, and fruitwoods imported from all over, no place not some other place, nor is there any fitting in, for fitness is the optical effect, the fruit of cobbled parts.

The problem—which Penelope well knew when she told the dream of her husband's return to Odysseus, disguised as a homeless wanderer—is that "dreams are hard to unravel, wayward, drifting things." Some are true and some are false, and there are two ways you know: they wander either through the gates of ivory or gates of horn. Through ivory, and "their message bears no fruit," a stunted tree.

But some dreams can be made true. After his wanderings, the French Romantic Chateaubriand bought a small estate at Aulnay with money he made writing novels like *René* and *Atala*, which he characterized as "the products of my dreams and my waking hours"—that is, of wilding, bewildering day-dreams. At Aulnay, his home in political exile, Chateaubriand planted many different varieties of trees from his travels all over the world, in Greece, Asia Minor, Palestine, Egypt, Tunisia and Spain, which is the reason he wrote in his memoirs that "[i]t is to the great wilderness of *Atala* that I owe the little wilderness of Aulnay."

Little transplanted wilderness of real pine, real fir, real larch and cedar, fig and oak, maple and ivory, hemp and iron, pitch and horn, oil and apple, pallets and turbines. To wander, like a dream, or a room of wood, from the woods of written dreams into the wooded world. So which one is it? Have I pitched through horn, or pined through ivory?

And into whose mind? Who is that wakes, and takes in at a golden angle their shallow room for one of swarming depth?

Is it mine?

Haul

"The great gifts are not got by analysis. Everything good is on the highway." / Ralph Waldo Emerson

Before I fully register what I'm looking at—a strip with little images of fruit that lines the lower border of a semi-trailer—we pass the rig on its left. It recedes behind us at a passive rate. B and I continue on into the slow roll of Wyoming high-country on our way from Utah to Colorado.

There was a similar trim where the walls met ceiling in the house that I grew up in: a paper border with panels of bright yellow pears, grape clusters, winter apples. The bedroom I shared with my brother was papered with one, too, though more foliate, venous, less fruited. For years my mother wanted to replace this bedroom border with a nautical, maritime theme: ships' wheels, barrels, gulls, telescopes. Despite her intentions to decorate with mercantile tropes, my room's interior imagery never progressed beyond the agricultural phase. I remained arborescent, autochthonous. Or maybe I should say that I remain. For, as the philosopher Gilles Deleuze writes, "there is always a way of reterritorializing oneself in the voyage: it is always one's father or mother (or worse) that one finds again on the voyage."

The train from Salt Lake to Provo, which I take from the airport to attend my brother's wedding, opens a vein through northern Utah's industrial corridor. Along the way, you can watch a procession of low-ceilinged storage facilities, foundries, warehouses, stone wholesalers, scrap-yards. Just off work, a commuter sits across from me and plays a video game on his phone before sliding into a light nap. Between Lehi and Orem, since it runs parallel to the freight line, our train draws up alongside and keeps pace with what feels like miles of tanker and hopper cars, as well as some empty platforms and some flatbeds stacked with plastic-wrapped particleboard.

The commuter wakes and watches the paneling of train. He chats for a while with some men sitting across the aisle, and they wonder about the contents of the freight cars. The commuter says he has a friend in the shipping business who would transport bulk quantities of milk in a tanker car going north, then carry gas in the same car south. Between loads, they would steam-clean the interior so that gas didn't get into the milk.

"Of course, you can't get everywhere," he adds. "Think of the nooks and crannies you'd have to reach in there."

Overhearing this, I suddenly imagine the inside of a tanker car no longer as a smooth cylinder, but as a topological crumple, full of divots and crevices. A body of seams and rims and rivets and edges where parts-per-million milk or gas get trapped. An uncleanable interior. A receding-from-everything, spiking and folding into itself.

That taste in your mouth is you. You can't get rid of it. Nor your internal topography of nooks and crannies and rooms and deeper rooms.

Deleuze, again: "In fleeing everything, how can we avoid reconstituting both our country of origin and our formations of power, our intoxicants, our psychoanalyses and our mummies and daddies?"

The first artistic representation of string beans ever appears in the scrolling, illuminated margins of a book of hours painted by Jean Bourdichon in 1515. The illustrations, made to beautify the texts of prayers, also feature foxglove, lilies of the valley, dragonflies, the tip of the wing of which glides just across the frame of the border, breaking hyper-realistically into the space of the psalm: *"Seven times a day I praise you for your righteous laws."*

Bourdichon uses the imagery of abundance as an accompaniment of praise. By ornamenting a prayer of praise, the string beans and dragonflies and other good things of this world participate in that prayer's purpose. In Bourdichon's hands, form itself becomes a form of praise, praise of law that form is.

To praise the poets, crown them with a wreath from the laurel tree.

Pricked by the gold-tipped arrow of Eros, Apollo gave chase to Daphne, a nymph promised to Chastity. Daphne, pursued, prayed to her father Peneus once it became apparent that Apollo would stop at nothing to possess her: "Open the earth to enclose me, or change my form, which has brought me into this danger!" So foot into root, root into ground. So branches are snapped and plaited together to crown the poets, who also stop at nothing, who also hunger and thirst to no end, who have to stop at something, who are rebuffed once the object of their desire retreats into the form of an actual object, recedes into the world, into the borders, the overgrowth.

The object, always an object of desire, escapes into form—in this case, the form of a tree. Instead of consummation, now you have materials with which to adorn, to honor and praise those who sing the songs of desire.

By virtue of their virtual reality, Bourdichon's images of abundance are encoded with desire—a desire for the real dragonfly, the real bean. The things of this world dwell in the margins and the borders, unbordering the text, which, here, is a prayer in praise of law. The dragonfly is quick, quickened into itself. The hours are long. To pass the time, I catalogue the company names of the trucks on the freeway. Stevens Transport. Illy. Prime Inc. ABF. FedEx. Xtreme Leasing. Killer "B" Trucking. Forward Air. Crown Group. Greatwide. CR England. R and R Transportation. Mercer Transportation. YRC Freight. Atlantic and Pacific Freightways. KLLM. Werner Enterprises. John Christner Trucking. CRST Expedited. Toad Transport. Crete Carrier.

I keep an eye out for a truck with the same port-side border that I spotted earlier. The next time I see it, I want to study it more closely. But my search is fruitless. All I have is this other, endless list.

B will start his MFA in documentary filmmaking at Northwestern in the fall. As we snake the scenic byways of northern Utah, then arc into Wyoming, I tell him that my trouble with film is I can't quote it. My problem is it eludes reference in my writing. It feels like it is already its own thing. Fully imaged, imagined. Resistant to extraction.

As soon as the hand closes around a piece of fruit, and plucks it from the branch, the fruit metamorphoses from a living organism to a dead object— the stuff of a still life, a *nature morte*. It can be placed on a kitchen table. It can be arranged as a means to beautify.

I ask B what it is about film, for him, as medium. He answers that he loves the motion, movement. He answers that he moved around a lot as a kid, trucked from place to place and state to state by his parents in the back of a minivan. He came to love the world in all its slippery variety. A banner unfurling from a window, looking out. Compounding forms of movement—the movement of the shot, the movement of the plot—film reproduces for my friend his lived experience. On the move, everything quickening-in, the rest receding.

Though film is hard for me, B and I agree on the importance of the documentary and long-form journalism. After all, the actual world is all we have to work with. In an age of big data and its endless, endlessly available amassment, it seems impossible, or irresponsible, to fathom anything that isn't.

And anything that isn't should stay that way. Because there is enough of it already.

Enough already.

Bushels of multi-colored coolant tubes bob between the prime mover and the trailer of the semi-trucks we pass.

In the kinds of documentary we agree we like, what is in the background is what is at issue. Take, for instance, this jar of salsa on the gift and souvenir shelves at the Little America truck-stop in Sweetwater County, Wyoming. Why is it here? What drove the decision to stock this brand? The jar says it was manufactured in Kentucky. There is also a Bible verse printed on the label which goes, *the heavens are thine, the earth also is thine: as for the world and the fulness thereof, thou hast founded them.*

As we look at the jars of salsa and pickled quail eggs and jalapeños, B tells me about John Wilson, one of his favorite documentarians, who made a short film called "The Spiritual Life of Wholesale Goods" that looks in part at the curious practice of printing proverbs and words of wisdom on packaging for mass-produced items like plug-in air fresheners or rolls of solid steel galvanized wire. Above a note of copyright the manufacturer observes: "Without the appreciation of kindness, society breaks down." Above a bar code: "Be forgiving toward others. Be discreet in your speech." Wilson's idea is to try and trace the moral values that inform corporate production in America. What drives production beyond, outside of, production itself.

The reality is we know nothing about this apple butter. Everything about it is in the background. It falls to the documentarian to bring it all forward. To establish a lineage. The provenance of provender. The wormhole that the search for the roots of plenty can become. The apple that forms around the hole. There flourishes a laurel tree, the writer's prize, where some other object was desired.

B records some of our trip on his MiniDV camcorder. Because he hasn't figured out how to take the video off the camera and onto his laptop, B uses the view-screen to show me some footage from a few months prior, scrubbing through shots of: a Standing Rock protest on Hollywood Boulevard; the super bloom, families in sun-visors bending down to take photos in its midst; the interior of an L.A. mansion, chandeliers, headless busts, angel statues on the landings; a woman trying on a pair of virtual reality goggles, ducking and reeling drunkenly into the images she must be seeing. As I watch I notice on the surface of the LCD screen the whorl of B's thumbprint. His overlay of oils, unguents. His issue. The foregrounder that he is.

Forward Air. Greatwide. Shuttler. Trucker. Eater of the road.

In the spring of 1842, a young Henry David Thoreau remarked in his journal, "How simple is the natural connection of events. We complain greatly of the want of flow and sequence in books, but if the journalist only move himself from Boston to New York, and speak as before, there is link enough. Is not my life riveted together? Has not it sequence? Do not my breathings follow each other naturally?"

For Thoreau, the body is enough of a transporter. The lung is the long form of journalism. Breathe, and there are rivets. Look, and you are riveted.

I guess I can't help it. This growing not-knowing. For my very existence is sequence, is synthesis, and synthesis is riveting. And along those rivets, in the heads and seams of the flush, there is nothing I can do about what gets caught in there, what recedes from reach inside me, and roots. What milk, what gas, what oils and unguents. In there, it blooms and re-blooms, that border of flowers and fruit, the overgrowth that obscures me from myself, until the self itself is a kind of tree, and with it I will wreathe and sing and wreathe.

Likes

A group of doves perched on the lip of a filled bowl is used in Roman tomb art to symbolize the dead and their thirst. Though widespread in its Roman usage, the image originates with the Greek mosaicist Sosso, who showed, according to the philosopher Pliny the Elder, "a dove taking a drink, darkening the water with the shadow of its head; others bask in the sun while grooming themselves at the edge of a basin."

By leaning down to water's surface, the dove drinks from the darkness of its drinking.

The mosaicist Sosso is described as an early practitioner of the *trompe l'oeil*—that is, the art of the "trick of the eye," a style of rendering the unreal real—or all but—so characteristic of still life painting.

I have started to see still life everywhere. The day cools, the room darkens, depths flourish, and objects arranged by chance and life and use become evidence of the presence of that life, and, in becoming evidence of presence, become bounteous. In my own kitchen, even: chopped carrots, fresh corn cubed from its cob, half a yellow onion in a plastic Ziploc bag. All piled on top of a cutting board with a decal image in its lower left-hand corner of a cornucopia of vegetables.

In the evening light, even the smallest kernel of corn casts a long shadow along the cutting board. I try to take a picture of this effect with my iPhone. At first, leaning over the scene, my shadow obscures the finer chiaroscuro. I have to move out of the way and take the photo at an angle, then account for that angle as I edit later, when I post it effortlessly for everyone, first adding filters to make the shadows deeper.

Look. I was here. I was hungry.

A cooler, wetter winter in Southern California has precipitated this spring a super bloom. Seeds that have long been dormant in the dead earth—the seeds of California poppies, desert sunflowers, dune evening primroses, sand verbena, ghost flowers, wild Canterbury bells, ocotillo and beavertail cactus—have been activated in rare conditions, flourishing into endless mosaics of color along the slopes and up the canyon mouths. The super bloom could recede again into heat-crisped thistles and twigs in just a matter of days. As soon there as not. News services report a mass exodus into the desert. Families in sun-visors swarm into the arid L.A. hills to snap selfies to prove they were there, leaning with cameras over the colorful extent, impossible to fully capture. Authorities warn about traffic jams and the risks of dehydration, sunstroke. Parks and Recreation prophesies a long summer of wildfire, the unframable turning flammable.

If the dead are thirsty, they thirst for all that they had once. They thirst for what they drank. That is to say, they thirst because they drank. When the dead thirst, they thirst for thirsting. They thirst for a sense that helps them know they lack, that they must be restored, too much salt in the bloodstream, which is more than knowing—that is to say, is less than knowing, because the body does not know, but is, and does, and must be. That is, until it isn't. What the dead thirst for is this unknowing. This pure knowledge so pure, so distilled, it is not aware of itself as such, is not self-reflexive, is given not to feedback, but to feedforward, the continuity of need and satisfaction.

John Keats knew this and lived a posthumous life because of it. In his "Ode to a Nightingale," the bird he hears is just a bird. This is its great happiness. It is happy—"too happy," says Keats—because it is not given to thinking, which is sorrow, which is when "men sit and hear each other groan," knowing, recognizing their own face in the faces of others, what it is that will befall them. Instead, the nightingale is given to its own givenness. It is self-given. There is no interval there. For the nightingale, there is no coming back to itself, because it was never gone. It never needed to be.

Be gone, I mean.

Keats spends the poem wishing he could leave himself. He thinks maybe a drink of wine might help him do that:

"O for a beaker full of the warm South,
    Full of the true, the blushful Hippocrene,
        With beaded bubbles winking at the brim,
            And purple-stained mouth;
    That I might drink, and leave the world unseen,
        And with thee fade away into the forest dim…"

Of course, in the poem, any time that Keats says he wants a drink so as to drink himself into oblivion, he can only say so by saying he wants something else. He can't just say he wants a fucking glass of wine. Instead, he wants to drink of "the warm South." He wants to taste of "Flora," a personage of spring and dance and song and mirth. He wants to taste the Hippocrene and also the "country green."

"Hippocrene" is the name of a fountain on Mount Helicon. In Greek it means "fountain of the horse," because it was formed from a stroke of Pegasus's hoof.

Henry David Thoreau says that the reason we love to hear the roaring of waterfalls and cataracts is that "it is allied to the circulation in our veins." Less a being of *telos*, of destiny, the human being is, according to Thoreau, more a continuous cascade, for "we have a waterfall which corresponds even to Niagara somewhere within us." If the person, a creature of blood, is a cataract, so also is the horse. So also is the nightingale, which pours forth song as a horse pours forth. When the dead thirst, they thirst for waterfalls. The Hippocrene of being. Its ceaseless feeding-forward.

Google's DeepDream software evolved out of a facial-recognition project that attempted to reduce the rate of error in programs designed to detect and organize scenes, images of objects, and human faces. Eventually, the software became better than humans at correctly telling what is what.

Maybe this shouldn't come as a surprise. Think of the tricks you play on yourself; the *trompe l'oeil* of the eye itself. Think of how many times you look up from the page of a book, stare into shadows cast by candlelight, and see in the shifting depths of the room a swirl of krill—though this is just your eyes adjusting, trying to make sense of what is barely—if not, not—there.

Seeing something that isn't there is called "pareidolia." The same result occurs when an image-recognition software runs in reverse, which researchers at Google discovered and then developed into DeepDream, a convolutional neural network that seeks out then enhances patterns in images that aren't actually there. If DeepDream is fed the image of jellyfish, all-but-translucent against a blue deep-sea backdrop, it will read into every curve and line and clot of pixels a world of possible connections and likeness, pulling on the vast visual library of the ImageNet to render what could be. What could be a seal with the beak of a dove. What could be a

Ferris wheel. What could be a lighthouse. What could be a city of lighthouses. What could be a lighthouse-keeper wearing rain-gear.

A convolutional neural network is designed to work like a brain. A cluster of algorithmic functions called "dendrites," it is non-linear, continuous, piecewise, differentiable, and bounded. It can develop threshold logics, or logic gates that perform operations on multiple binary inputs as a way of deriving a single output. When the inputs and outputs are mathematical functions, and when the output is a modified version of an original function, the result is called "convolution."

Convolutions can be cascaded. DeepDream is just such a cascade of convolutions. When it operates, it operates on a network principle of feed-forward, where the neural or algorithmic connections between units do not form a cycle. Convolutions redound into further convolutions. Algorithms are swallowed into algorithms. A jellyfish riffle develops into a seal that develops a dove-beak.

What isn't there is there as much as it could be.

And as soon as it's there, it's not.

Before the advent of refrigeration, in order to preserve your perishables, you stored them in cool cellars on cold stone surfaces. You used fine string to hang from the ceiling a head of cabbage or some apples.

Touching nothing, there is nowhere for fruit to fester and rot.

A variation on the stone-niche setting (popular in portrayals of surging, botanically exact bouquets of flowers), Juan Sánchez Cotán rendered a number of still life paintings whose context was a *canteraro*—that cool stone cellar shelf on which vegetables curved, or hung above, on strings, stilly, untouched, not touching.

Cotán, a Carthusian monk, liked to emphasize the geometric, formal beauty of his still-life victuals. Except for the plain stone niche in which they cooled, unconsumed, the rest of his paintings are occupied by shadow and darkness. You can see nothing in the background of *Still Life with Game Fowl, Vegetables and Fruits*. There is nothing there but game fowl, vegetables and fruits.

The asymptote of a bunch of white chard forms half of a parabola, carried through in the curvature of a pile of pale carrots.

During Cotán's lifetime, the Netherlandish provinces enjoyed an economic surge that meant an increased demand for art among the middle merchant class of the Dutch Republic, who, as a result of flourishing international trade, were newly possessed of disposable incomes with which they could represent themselves and their hard-won wealth and social status. A fine landscape or still life hanging in a hallway demonstrated prosperity and discriminating taste. It was not long before masters of the still life could so finely reproduce an import that realism began to border on abstraction, the really real of forms, less chard than gleaming curve.

A neural network can be harnessed to obviate the difficulties of face detection, where visual variations, like pose, expression, and lighting, call for a discriminative model that can differentiate faces from backgrounds. In a normal neural network, discriminative capacities develop out of the feedforward cascade of overlapped, then convoluted, then tiled inputs. To so overlay as to clarify.

A neural chiaroscuro. Where chiaroscuro adds depth. Where depth adds reality.

DeepDream takes its logic a step further. Once the network has so fed-forward, so trained to tell what is what—that is, what is the shadow of an inset eye, what is the shadow in a California poppy cupping up—what could be there is more there than what is.

What is there is what it is like.

After I feed and re-feed and feed again Juan Sánchez Cotán's *Still Life with Game Fowl, Vegetables and Fruits* into a DeepDream generator, the shadowy interior of the *canteraro* begins to adopt the metallic multicolored sheen of a common green bottle fly, or a peacock train. A greenish, mossy depth develops in the topmost gloom. The swoop of intervening blackness beneath the group of apples and hanging pheasants morphs into a furred, sinuous, eye-sheathed python, whose head expresses itself as the feathery, bilateral chest of a falcon, once a wall-propped skewer of taxidermic songbirds. The carrots are reptilian crustaceans. The apples and pheasants have been rounded and melted into vase-forms. There are human faces spliced in the lemons. Sand-pipers peek out from the heart of the chard. A bouquet of salmon-scales and ferret-bodies and baby-flesh and nightingale feathers burst forth from the fringes of the chard's trimmed shafts.

Nothing was never there.

Whenever J and I talk, talk always turns to the nineteenth-century American philosopher Charles Sanders Peirce and the nineteenth-century British poet John Keats, our respective patron thinkers. As we walk on a Sunday evening into the spring-thickened woodlands near the river, J describes some of his afternoon reading, in which Peirce makes the claim that a line is less an abstract infinity of points as much as a point is the continuity, in time, that a line is. For Peirce, the principle of continuity is prior to the geometric abstractions of either line or point. I point out that the reason we like to render our world into units as discrete as points and lines might be the same as the reason I like still life. The still life is a bounded, controlled, composed arrangement of objects. The still life satisfies a different hunger. It is the hunger not to have to eat what's in front of you. The hunger to sit back and appreciate. The hunger to eat for the sake of taste, which is the absence of hunger, which is the taking into my mouth a mouthful of wine, and picking apart the grapes, and saying, it's bright to me, it's buttery, it's charcoal, it's jammy, it's oaked, it's silky, it's steely, it's structured. To taste is to discriminate. To sense in fullness floral notes of what it is like.

In his essay "The Red and the Black," Peirce refers to the pre-Socratic Parmenides, who is known for saying that everything that is is, and everything that is not is not. Peirce qualifies Parmenides' aphorism with his own argument that what is probable is real. To this end he writes:

> "…in the long run, there is a real fact which corresponds to the idea of probability, and it is that a given mode of inference sometimes proves successful and sometimes not, and that in a ratio ultimately fixed. As we go on drawing inference after inference of the given kind, during the first ten or hundred cases the ratio of successes may be expected to show considerable fluctuations; but when we come into the thousands and millions, these fluctuations become less and less; and if we continue long enough, the ratio will approximate toward a fixed limit."

It would seem that Peirce had a finer sense of reality than Parmenides. For Peirce, part of the fact of the real is that it could be differently. That is, whatever is, is probably.

For Peirce, a forerunner of quantum physics, what is is like a bell curve. Is, parabolically.

But Peirce points out we never get the full bell-shape of any truth. Because people die, people do not have access to unlimited cases to ferret out the fluctuations of the fixed limit that anything has, given infinity:

> "All human affairs rest upon probabilities, and the same thing is true everywhere. If man were immortal he could be perfectly sure of seeing the day when everything in which he had trusted should betray his trust, and in short, of coming eventually to hopeless misery. He would break down, at last, as every good fortune, as every dynasty, as every civilization does. In place of this we have death."

That is, what we have is half a parabola. What we have is an asymptote.

Since each individual person suffers death, the individual person cannot reach the fact of reality. In light of this, Pierce says that the closest we can get to truth is through a continuity or an "unlimited" community of human thinkers. In this closeness is a "hope, or calm or cheerful wish, that the community may last beyond any assignable date." Hope in the hope that brings us thus closer, and still closer.

In the days that follow the super bloom, Facebook and Instagram also overflow, but with pictures captured in the laps of southern California valleys. Where there was once nothing has flourished a vast mosaic of bright cup-shapes that will wither then burst into flame come June and July. Now that something is there, there is danger.

To post a photo of the bloom provides the internet, or all of us, a finer sense of things.

A finer sense of what is like, and what is not.

With every photo, the dream warps closer to reality.

In the meantime, there are those who have risked sunstroke to rove the hills in Ray-Bans.

They are leaning out of the frame to get a good, unshadowed shot of a field of poppies, thinking of the likes they'll get.

Cognoscenti in a Room Hung with Pictures

1. *Still Life with Quince, Cabbage, Melon, and Cucumber,* Juan Sánchez Cotán

Quince and cabbage hang from the ceiling by string in a storage niche. Underneath, a cantaloupe has one-third cut away from it, exposing a clotted core of slick seeds. A slice rests beside the melon, but it is not enough to account for the missing portion; the remainder, I assume, has been eaten. Closest to the niche wall on the left, a cucumber extends across the edge of the stone shelf and scuffs a cross-lit shadow at an angle down the wall. So composed, food is elegized as form, plangent with light. The leading bow of the melon slice is so engulfed in sun it is transposed as sun itself, into pure absorptive surface. This painting, as well as others by the seventeenth century Carthusian monk Juan Sánchez Cotán, gives me a sense of austere repose. Cotán offers me food—I hunger, and he feeds me—but it is food excised of its associations with satiety or with emptiness. He feeds another hunger. The painting engages my senses, but abstracts them first from reflex, need, pain, pleasure. If I am hungry, to look at such a quince, at such a cantaloupe, is not to experience a moment of imaginative reprieve, but to eradicate the whole system of nerves and neurons that forms a hollow in the belly or goads the glands beneath my tongue.

When I am still hungry, I love to look at these paintings. I love how the space of my hunger is not filled, but instead swallowed up in a greater emptiness. It is why cathedrals were built. Under the high clerestory, in the void shaft of a rose window, the worshipper jumps a valence, climbs a rung. The arch of the niche in Cotán's cooling pantry is as high-vaulted as any at Cologne or Chartres, or at Saint Jean, in Lyon, beneath whose ribbing King Henry IV married Marie de Medici.

The cruelty of an image is that it excites us toward an anticipation that it can't fulfill. It gives by taking away. Though, when Cotán gives me an image of fruit, he does not take away from me any particular instance of pear or pomegranate—instead, he takes away the whole idea of fruit. It is as if I never as a child experienced the apple tree bent against the fence in my front yard, the knotted fruits of which were as dusty on the inside as the out.

And yet, part of the cantaloupe is gone. Someone has cut it away. Someone was here before me. And the ease with which they ate and left now disenchants me of Cotán's pious rinds and waxy ribs, and I remember that what I am looking at can in fact be eaten, someone after all has done it, and then I remember that it cannot be eaten, that after all it is oil on canvas and hangs in the San Diego Museum of Art.

2. *A la memoire de J.M. Jacquard né a Lyon le 7 juilliet 1752, mort le 7 aeout 1854, d'apres le tableau de C. Bonneford*, Didier Petit et Cie.

Using only a drawloom, the patterning of woven cloth is a difficult, labor-intensive process. A master and his apprentice work across the loom, raising by hand the heddle of each warp, choreographing the final stroke of each taut moment. Once the weft is shuttled in at a right angle, the two weavers lay a single thread of a final patterned image. It is as if the master weaver is the conductor of an orchestra paused in time: for every individual note from every individual instrument, he has to run between the frozen players, raising a bow here, an elbow there, has to blow air into a lung, massage it through the trachea so that it fills the embouchure of a frozen mouth pressed against a horn.

The Jacquard loom automated this process. Seeing it as a threat to their trade, silk-weavers destroyed prototypes of Jacquard's first loom in the streets of Lyon in 1801. The word "saboteur" comes to us from the wood *sabot*, the shoes that laborers like the Lyonnais weavers would either wear or throw into the delicate mechanism of a weaving machine.

Jacquard's invention was a synthesis of prior solutions by past inventors. Vaucanson's system of hooks and paper. Falcon's punchcards. By passing a continuous strand of punched paper or cardboard through a reading cylinder that controlled a system of drawstrings and hooks, a loom could be "programmed" to raise the desired warp threads and lower others, weaving tapestries and silks, brocades and damasks of exquisite detail and complexity. One such weaving is a portrait of Jean Marie Jacquard himself, executed by Michel-Marie Carquillat and the Lyon manufacturer Didier, Petit et Cie, who created a silk rendition of such extreme and close-set fineness that it became a favorite party trick of the English polymath Charles Babbage to convince his guests it was an engraving they were looking at in his private gallery. When he revealed that this portrait of Jacquard, procured from the manufacturer in 1840, was, in fact, a tapestry, he would add that by using Jacquard's punchcard technique he could at last perfect his own invention, the Analytical Engine, a not-yet-realized computing machine. By the turn of the twentieth century, using developments by Babbage, Jacquard, and others, the International Business Machines Corporation had begun manufacturing the tabulating apparatuses that would evolve into the modern computer.

In tapestry, image is actual structure. A silk tapestry shows a picture of an inventor in his workshop, a caliper in his hand, slippers on his feet, glass cracked in the window-panes and chisels lined along the wall—none of which would exist without that picture, laid down thread by thread. The method of manufacturing the structure and the image would not exist without what it images.

An image is real when it begins to realize itself, self-reflexive, when its medium is also what it represents. Thus made self-aware, artificially intelligent, the image is no longer an image. It is a machine. It machines other machines. A way of looking or thinking can be a machine, a kind of technology. A portrait in silk taught Babbage to look at it not as if it were a portrait but a matrix of possibility.

The limits of what I can do exist at the limits of my tools, but the tool through history is not a static object. Instead, it begets other, finer, more efficient tools that accomplish more or other ends. Without the Jacquard loom, there would be no punchcard system, and so no computer, and so no dwindling of the stevedore trade in city ports, where loading and offloading relies on increasing automation. Consider the mega-port at Busan. Look at the dockside gantries, the spreader, the twistlock, the daily sedimentation of the geologic unit that is the stackable intermodal container, shifting in rusting, multi-colored layers like shale—workings that cannot be known by one mind, are not known by a mind at all, but by an algorithm, whose labor is distributed across a server, or across many servers, and where these are cannot be fathomed either, much less the cables fathoms-deep that run along the ocean floor and flay data to the coasts.

What I can do, what there is to be done, changes. I am differently limited. The shifting of my limits limit others.

But I am only the weaver's apprentice. I am following a thread with my hand, I am following a thought to its most distant or outlandish conclusion, its odd end. I lift it into position, shuttle in the weft, try to figure a pattern. The threads of the image comprise the structure that supports the image, emerging gradually, an expression of alternating linearities. And like Babbage, like Jacquard, my work is a working out of work that has come before. One work is the substructure for another. And not just the work itself, but how it is made, the *technē*, taught me. In this manner, I am tasked to a contraption of flounces, of forces.

3. *Pie Fight Interior 11*, Adrian Ghenie

Immortalized in Dante's *Inferno,* Francesca and Paolo's sin started with pornography. Looking at others in their throes, my own capacity for desire increases. There is now a threshold there that was not there before. A doorframe plus a door. I enter but realize the fact of my crossing only after, seeing only now behind me the lintels and posts, the fanlight, walls rising around me, just as Paolo and Francesca da Rimini must have traced the threshold of their first embrace back to that erotica, the Old French romance *Lancelot du Lac*. Thanks to a book that taught them to love, they now fly forever in a vortex of desire. This room, too, is a chaos. Or it is a *kunstkammer,* a cabinet of curiosities, a room of odds and ends, and on the drafts of wind carried through it (from an open window in the bottom left-hand corner) there are other blown souls reciting their desires. There are others there to witness those witnesses, as in the anonymous Flemish painting *Cognoscenti in a Room Hung with Pictures*, painting of a gallery of paintings and prints by Dürer and Lucas van Leyden, and the Antwerp artists of the 16th and 17th centuries, including works in the style of Joachim Beuckelaer, Joos de Momper, Jan Brueghel the Elder and Frans Francken.

A desire, like a machine, machines further desire. A desire is a desiring-machine. It learns or works by punchcard, voids and holes fed into it that guide where the needle goes and what pattern accumulates. What portrait.

Here is a portrait:

In the long days leading up to this morning, I have followed P around Paris, taking snapshots of broken eggs in standing street-water or of vacant storefronts with windows washed white on the inside. She wears Adidas, neon leggings and a denim jacket, and stalks the sideroads at a bent. A conversation with P crazes from gut-flora, to Deleuze and Guattari, to the industrial sublime. On first meeting, we bond over a shared love of the blue tarps bound with bungee cords to stacks of baled hay—a common sight in the southern Oregon countryside we both call home. P loves bales for the same reason she loves pallets, forklifts. Logistics, she insists. The geodesic vectors of the global supply chain. Stacks. Shipping containers. Warehouses. Robert Moses. Hard water. Soft money. Usage of this word "logistics" can be traced back to the Napoleonic complex of factors involved in large-scale troop movement. It comes from the French *loger*, for "quartering" or "lodging." A "loge" is a spectator's box in a theater. A *corps de logis* is a section of a palace, as in, that wing designed as gallery space to house Peter Paul Reubens' Marie de Medici cycle—the apologia-apotheosis of the widow of Henry IV, the Protestant-now-Catholic king who declared *"Paris veut bien une messe."*

A kingdom for just a taste.

Here is a portrait:

P uses her index finger to lick spilled sugar off an outdoor table at a cafe on the Rue des Archives. I am thinking back to the Adrien Ghenie I saw at the Pompidou: *Pie Fight Interior 11*, a figure in a house-dress stooping at a dark bureau table, her face half-sunk in crème fraîche dabs of pastel paint. Her gluttony is focused and abject. Or perhaps she is trying to wipe her face clean. Ghenie's other pie fight interiors reiterate this gesture: figures with smeared faces lift their hands to wipe off the spattered excess, the meringue of whipped buildup, and—caught in that action—are shown with their palms to their cheeks. They might as well be mid-scream.

Ghenie's work has been described as baroque, opaque, and immanent, or closed off and entire to themselves. While his paintings may refer to personal memories—textures, debris, postures inflected by the shadows of specific spaces—or to historical sources, these allusions are assimilated and transformed by the re-worlding that his work performs. Surfaces accrete. Succulence compounds, fractures, dehiscent. Like Leibniz's monad, which supports no direct point of access—all room, all cellule, vessel—the interior becomes autonomous, an inside without an outside. Ghenie's interiors are digestive chambers. The gut with its world, its colonies of microbial flora.

This is the problem of the interior. It keeps interiorizing. Much as in the Baroque painting *Cognoscenti in a Room Hung with Pictures*, completed in Flanders in the 1620s—the image exists as a framework for other images; its world, for other worlds. It is a work that reflects widespread attitudes toward art in the Dutch and Flemish contexts. Art was a means to index, to record, to botanize, to arraign nature in all its many forms, even as it also was intended to beautify, adorn, and be possessed as icons of knowledge and human grace by private collectors and gallerists.

A work, then, of the hyper-baroque, in *Cognoscenti in a Room Hung with Pictures* the gallery is festooned with points of access, each painting a window, a window fractalizing into further windows.

The desire to contain gets out of hand.

After breakfast, in our rented flat on Rue Oberkampf, I am naked in P's hand. By noon, I have lost my virginity and am drifting through the Pompidou, looking for a framework. I, like the cognoscenti, use frames as tools to try to understand. To go in and in and in.

4. Parthenon, East Frieze

Desire gets out of hand. It is out of my hands.

Headquartered in Indianapolis, Celadon Trucking has one of its satellite terminals in Henderson, Colorado. The company has signaled it intends to report a 10-million-dollar operating loss this year. The new COO, heir ascendant to the family dynasty following the death of his father, says he plans to fix the problem by going back to the "basics of trucking." Less leasing and outsourcing. Shorter dwell times. Smaller, better distributed terminal towns. Higher pay in areas of high freight density. J and I walk single-file up the road shoulder beside the loading bay at the Coors factory in Golden, thirty miles southwest of the Henderson outfit.

My aim is to make a circuit around the perimeter, feel close to industry, set my cheek against its haunch, the small of it, where it tapers toward the ribcage. I point out to him the Celadon logo in the lot and tell him about the glaze-type developed on the Korean peninsula during the Goryeo and Joseon dynasties. When Steve Russell and Lee Bennett named their company, they had this same pottery glaze in mind. They hoped their business would grow to become just as "distinctive."

The commerce trail between the US and Mexico starts on a New York toll-bridge in the 80s, where Russell comes up short fifty cents; he has the money, just not the coin. Bennett, an old employee, happens to see his ex-boss pulled over on the roadside. He also sees an opportunity and pitches his idea to Russell for a logistics company. He even has a client already in hand, a job hauling car parts down to the Chrysler factory in Mexico.

In his inaugural address, Donald Trump paints a panorama of multiple worlds, insisting that, in America, "...a different reality exists: Mothers and children trapped in poverty in our inner cities; rusted-out factories scattered like tombstones across the landscape of our nation; an education system, flush with cash, but which leaves our young and beautiful students deprived of knowledge; and the crime and gangs and drugs that have stolen too many lives and robbed our country of so much unrealized potential."

Trump sums up this different reality as a world of "American carnage." Manichean wars seethe in the substratum.

Eight hundred years ago, a scholar in China's southern Song Dynasty called celadon glaze "the best under heaven." Outside the Coors factory, J tells me that celadon is the same brand-type of American Spirit that his wife H smokes, half a cigarette at a time. J, on the other hand, takes a full ten minutes with a single menthol, sitting when it rains on top of a plastic grocery bag out on the porch-bench.

I have lived with H and J as their roommate for two and a half years. I have chosen to wade out into the dissolution of their marriage, let it tug at my ankle and in that riptide think what it might be like to give myself over to it. These days, H has Tim, a stage-magician down in Denver, and J has fallen in love with Andrea, a lanky cos-player and autodidact in quantum mechanics and the philosophy of science. They met in a grad seminar on analytic formal tools at Colorado State. Epistemic modal logic. Decision Theory. Virtual quanta. There is a stylized phoenix printed on the paper of every American Spirit cigarette. Every object is a totem of desire.

After smoking her half cigarette, H comes back inside from the stoop, brushes her teeth, sprays Febreze in the stairwell and in what she calls our "foyer." In fact, it is little more than an access space between bedrooms where we store our bicycles. I try to imagine what H (whose heart's hornbook is *A Lover's Discourse*, by Roland Barthes) thinks of when she says or hears this word "foyer".... The intimacy of thresholds? seduction in a doorframe? the tedium of voices barely audible through a buffer of Sheetrock and fiberglass?

Desire is a domestic architecture. Shadows dwell. Eaves, brackets, fanlights, and terraces are expressions of the constraints and airy sunrooms of love, of shifts in attention, diurnal rotations, that transpire over the course of an affair. Spandrels of consequence and distraction form where walls and ceilings meet. Bas-reliefs in rosewood. The bathtub develops claw-feet.

Andrea leaves town to visit Greece for three weeks, and, since he is always tracking his position in the world relative to hers, a new fold ruffs across the surface of J's geodesy. Andrea texts J videos showing fragments of the Parthenon, which he in turn shows me in my bedroom on his phone. In June, I go to London and, in the British Museum, same as John Keats did, I see the Elgin marbles, among them the other half of the Parthenon frieze, which I record and send via text to J. When Keats looked at the torso of Iris, and shards of the shoulders of the sun god as he breaks the surface of the ocean of dawn, he was looking at "A sun—a shadow of a magnitude." I am forced to turn my eyes from the source of my world's light. I know my sources only through their shadows, the shadows of their magnitude.

In simple terms, a magnitude is the extent to which a cause effects a system. Timothy Morton, the Romanticist scholar turned prophet of the eco-apocalypse, writes about the advent of "objects" of unimaginable magnitude whose effects distribute massively across time. To describe this phenomenon, he has coined the word "hyperobject." Planets, global warming, plutonium particles, and Styrofoam coffee cups are all hyperobjects— though Morton also admits that "[i]n a strange way, every object is a hyperobject." Every object is, to some degree, "non-local," "viscous" or sticky, "interobjective" or meshed, its effects and presence distributed over time and space. In the case of extreme examples like polystyrene or plutonium, decaying at a glacial pace, these objects exist at timescales and in futures and in pasts that contain or frame and swallow up more human temporal frameworks—the timespan of a life, say, or of recorded history.

Morton shows how his is an Einsteinian model of objecthood. Einstein theorized that a mass will warp and marble spacetime, withdrawing or burrowing into it, creating limpet-like "world tubes": dimples of time and space that attract other objects of lesser magnitudes to dwell toward them as toward the variable depths of an eddy. Like a black hole, though to an infinitesimal extent, an American Spirit cigarette distributes itself and its gravity well through spacetime. An object is an object relative to its sphere of influence. A cigarette is a world tube. It has a light-cone and a timeframe I cannot conceive.

A cigarette is a pretext. For H, it is a symbol of discreet surrender to impulse. In the midwestern spirit of casseroles, darning, moderation, when H craves, she attends to, she nurtures that craving. Sprays deodorizer behind her, domesticates the desire. Dwells with it. It is incorporated into a genealogy of small sins, a family tree of them. For J, the cigarette started as a pretext to be on the porch. At first with H, then later with Andrea. Smoking a cigarette, which he once described to me as wings opening up inside the chest—a butterfly stroke into the intertide of time—became a ritual of love, then still later a way of holding out, of persisting inside an unrealized unreality. Andrea doesn't realize that I am what she wants, he says to me, again.

One of the cognoscenti, dressed in brocaded yellow silk, standing at the table by the window burdened with globes and comprehensive intricate tools for geo-positioning, shows so I can see it a small-scale picture with its cover slid to reveal a study of snails and insects. "Reference-mollusk" is another term that Einstein used to describe the world tube that an object is in spacetime, the mollusk's time-flesh the slippery Gaussian distribution of its attractive influence. Called *naturalia*, small paintings like this one of snails, proffered by a cognoscenti, occupied an important place in the sixteenth and seventeenth-century collection: renditions of the world, they were interchangeable with natural objects themselves. It less an object's presence that makes it real as much as it is my desire for it. It is my desire for it. My dwelling-toward, falling-for.

A vector is a magnitude plus a velocity. The speed light goes here. The shadows of time cast by the marble fragment of a surfacing sun god. I could go so far as to claim that desire is reality. But nothing is ever real or true on the basis of knowing it or claiming so. Instead, it is real as much as it is in the periphery. In terms of *Cognoscenti in a Room Hung with Pictures*, it is the monkey at the open casement window. Just below, there is an elder seated with a compass drafting tool trying to measure distance on a map. For a time, the Dutch were the masters of the world. Able to economize and judge time and distances with accuracy, they could orchestrate a vast logistics of international trade. Their shipping ports bristled with mastheads and tangled with rigging.

In a niche of shadows, a Dutch still-life of a painted bouquet interlaces spacetimes by depicting blossoms in the same vase that normally exist in opposite quadrants of the globe and during different seasons of the year. The world of the painting collapses the world.

Some of these still life masterpieces hang in the room with the cognoscenti, in a painting that is not about accuracy, but the desire for it, for the acquisition of a perfect knowledge. A desire to have the best under heaven all in one room. The mechanism of the world is to teach us to desire it. It is through the world we are programmed to want it. The more world there is, the more it is missing, a slice of cantaloupe.

In a tiny rented studio on Rue Oberkampf, my shoulder bangs some of the frames off the wall. They fall across my naked back. It is almost painful to submit to the pleasure.

Wolf Interval

Nothing is without a reason. But sometimes the reason is so simple it can't be understood. Meaning, it can't be analyzed or broken down to parts. This is how Leibniz proceeds: thinking is when some thoughts give rise to infinite other thoughts in order. But first those first thoughts have to think themselves. Thoughts like God, or Nothing. These go on self-thinking. "Although there is no hope," the philosopher wrote in 1679, "that men can, in this life, reach this hidden series of things, by which it will appear in what way everything comes from pure being and from nothing, it is sufficient to carry the analysis of ideas as far as the demonstration of truths require."

Thank God, I guess. Truth requires only so much. We can round up, rest, relax at home in things.

But there is a room in the house of knowledge for which there is no door. It is the room next to the room you grew up in. It is hung within with pictures you will never look at. Now, leave your room. Now leave your house. Now you are outside. What do you see.

I am on the back deck, looking out. In the middle distance of the yard, a fence, overgrown blackberry brambles shouldering into it. What do you see, who or what is out there, moving in that density. To me it is like the entire green is moving. I see a shoulder, the black glisten of an eye: a low, insinuating shape that has always lived among the tangled cane, but which I'd never noticed there before.

But why, given a blackberry, irreducible cluster, is reducing all I wanted to do to it? To pick it, and see if I can pick it apart, drupelet by drupelet, in lieu of eating it.

The problem with analysis, says Leibniz, is that it is limited to a single problem, to discrete contingencies; general principles do not follow. A further problem is that there is no such thing as pure analysis, "for when we look for means we often come across devices which have already been discovered either by others or by ourselves, whether by chance or by reason. These we find, whether in our own memory or in the accounts of others, as in a table or inventory, and we apply them to the matter in hand; and this is a synthetic procedure." Here Leibniz describes the reflex, as if muscular, toward synthesis. In the act of dismantling, it is all I can do to keep from putting back together.

The problem with analysis is that the matter in hand is a red smash.

The Baroque differs from Classical style in that it abandons symmetry and favors sinuosity, or curves that don't conclude. Walk around *Mercury* in a gallery and the outstretched body shifts and ranges in the several stages of its *contrapasto*.

In any new romance, you perceive yourself from different angles. You start to see how stuck you are like this. How real the limits of your own self-perception. But these are only glimpses you are getting. As soon as you catch sight of them, you continue to turn away from your own edges the way a piece of fruit spheres away in air.

At the outset of our relationship, K says, I never want to hurt you. The problem with that, I say back on our drive home from a concert, is what we are now to each other. The risk of synthesis has always been proximity: connections that weren't there that are there now. A small bone grows in empty spaces. A house burns in the night and a fireman gets his breastbone mashed. In François Truffaut's movie *Jules et Jim*, a meditation on how proximities dissolve into disaster, Jules stands on a balcony, looks down at Jim and Catharine in love on a lower level, recites some German verse out loud, and prompts Catharine to translate:

Catherine: "Hearts yearning for each other. O God O God. The pain they cause."
Jules: Not bad. Though "O God O God" was your addition.

The danger of synthesis has always been further synthesis.

Diagonals of light predominate the stained-glass scenes in the Hayes Barton United Methodist Church. In one window on the right-hand side of the chapel, Peter covers his face beside a rooster. Is he ashamed by what he has done, or that he knew he would do it?

At the front of the chapel, the Baroque Orchestra tunes itself to the harpsichord. As it turns out, each song will start out like this, preluded by an endless interval of tuning, loosening, retightening. During intermission, the conductor explains to the audience that this is because the catgut strings of period instruments are more sensitive to ambient factors, the August humidity. What's more, the temperaments used by Baroque composers gave greater range of expression but require elaborate and unfamiliar tuning systems. Each set has its own synchrony.

Sometimes I realize where I am and forget how I arrived. The strings slip. I have to remind myself why I'm listening to Telemann, Pisandel, and Rameau in a United Methodist church in Raleigh next to a person from Louisiana who loves Whitman so much she finds it hard to say anything about him, because that would ruin it, the effect, the tenuous sense of wholeness you get, the sudden apprehension, the way sunlight tilts through the nightlong frost come morning, lighting it through like a double world, a brilliance that promises its total ruin next. Yes, I remember—it is because I love the interplay between structure and excess, excess that turns to structure. The fantasia on a theme that becomes more thematic than the theme itself.

During the fifteenth and sixteenth centuries, the quarter-comma meantone temperament was widely used to establish major thirds that were "sonorous and just, as united as possible." Unlike equal temperament, which grew more popular during the Baroque and subsequent eras, the ratiocination of meantone temperaments like the quarter-comma makes for purity in all but eleven of a twelve-interval octave. However, in order to achieve this effect, existing tonal or rational impurity has to be bracketed off into one of the twelve intervals, where the distances between semitones become wider than in the other, more perfect intervals. This interval is called the "wolf." In modern equal temperament systems, impurities are shared across the range of an octave, sacrificing pure rational consonance in favor of harmonic possibility.

For the composers of the Renaissance, a desire for pure intervals was as much metaphysical as it was aesthetic in nature. The existence of pure Pythagorean intervals meant that nature operated on the basis of a dynamic holism, of radical rules and eternal ratios. The danger of harmony is the loss of purity, the loss of a pure ground of being. The danger of purity is the threat of a wolf. The wolf that is out there, lurking in the brambles.

I can only feel so much, but what I feel I swear I feel deeply. This is how I rationalize my strictures and limits, how cold I am to her, feel I have to be. In marble, the long continuity of a metamorphic vein moves against the new curve introduced in it, a sculpted arm outstretched. There is a reason I am like this, frost in a field, and on the thistles and the brambles by the fence. But then oblivion comes each morning in the form of deforming light. The sense of wholeness I thought I had, the sense of purity, now it's no more than moisture melted and swept up by her hemline as she crosses, cuts her kitty-corner line.

There is a field now that she is there. Is over there, traversable to. Now there is a space, empty place, a room, room to move around in, rotate, a bone grows. A table, an inventory, a bed, I struggle to stay awake. The strings slip, undone. Light at a tilt, fall light, cooler nights. She asks in my ear, what is it about the smell of woodsmoke and the night. Now there is an inside and an out. Now you can feel yourself inside yourself. Now you are home.

Or maybe there is no reason. Or maybe there is now none, having forgotten. The kind of singing that is like half-singing, cleaning, motes with sunbeams swirling in. A forgetting-the-song-as-I-sing-it kind of song...

Cryptography

My Life had stood - a Loaded Gun -
In Corners - till a Day
The Owner passed - identified -
And carried Me away -

And now We roam in Sovreign Woods -
And now We hunt the Doe -
And every time I speak for Him
The Mountains straight reply -

/ Emily Dickinson

On his trip to Italy in 1689, Gottfried Wilhelm von Leibniz prepared his selected universal library—a 35-page catalogue of must-have books. This bibliography included a dozen items on steganography, cryptology, and verbal concealment. Perhaps these books accompanied him as he traveled to Modena, in search of a common origin for the northern Italian House of Este and the German House of Brunswick-Lüneburg.

On my trip to Pittsburgh to see Leibniz's cipher machine—the first of two existing reconstructions of the philosopher's device, never once built in his lifetime—I bring with me two books: a hardbound art-edition of the Voynich Manuscript, and a copy of James Joyce's story, "The Dead." My copy of the Voynich has glossy, fold-out photo reproductions of the original manuscript's pages, which are filled with a curly cipher script accompanied by strange, rude images of unspeakable plants, bathing women, and cosmological signs and devices. Housed today in Yale's Beinecke Library, the original Voynich was written on parchment that dates from the early fifteenth century. Though many have tried, including American codebreakers who solved important encryptions during World War II, no one has been able to read or decipher the language in which the book is written—an alphabet of either 15 or 40 characters that scholars have called "Gallows" for the hangman-shaped style of its lettering. Nobody knows what the Voynich says, or if it says anything. Some think it was written as an elaborate con; during the Renaissance, both rare books and cryptography were much in vogue, and therefore ripe for counterfeit.

Some believe the book was written and encoded by Roger Bacon, a medieval Franciscan scientist, and then later taken from England to Prague by John Dee, a mathematician and alchemist who spoke to angels and knew well the theories of Johannes Trithemius—this latter, who, in addition to writing the first book on cryptography in Western Europe, proposed that people might be able to communicate with each other over long distances by using spirits. In Prague, the Holy Roman Emperor, Rudolph II, a lover of all things strange and uncommon, of genetic aberrations and curiosity cabinets, paid a small fortune to possess the manuscript for himself. After a long period of historical silence, the Voynich resurfaced in 1912, when it was purchased by a book dealer named Wilfrid M. Voynich, "a man of 'amazing bibliographical erudition' and 'almost omniscient knowledge,' who was said to be fluent in twenty different languages." He spent much of his life trying to decode the cipher manuscript. As part of his attempt, Voynich enlisted the help of William Romaine Newbold, a prominent medievalist at the University of Pennsylvania.

Newbold eventually claimed to have discovered the key to Bacon's cipher: each letter had to be "read" under a microscope, since each character was comprised of multiple parts or signs. Each sign on each letter was an abbreviation in Greek that could then be expanded into words, phrases, and entire paragraphs written in Latin. Even though Newbold was able to provide proof that portions of the Voynich could, in fact, be read in this way, he was ultimately proven wrong—what Newbold had seen under the microscope hidden in each letter of the manuscript was, in reality, cracks in the aging ink. John Matthews Manley, a codebreaker and English professor at the University of Chicago, explained why Newbold was able to produce legible solutions to the Voynich's encryptions on the basis of an impossible cipher-key, writing that "experience has shown that even a group of less than fifty letters can be rearranged in several thousand different ways all forming intelligible human speech." By Manley's logic, it wasn't so strange, then, that ink cracking over time might randomly reveal fragments of sensible language—in this case, an elaborate combination of Greek abbreviations unfurling into Latin paragraphs.

As we make the seven-hour trip to Pittsburgh, K and I alternate between driving and reading out loud from scholarly editorials written about the Voynich, and from James Joyce's "The Dead." I return to Joyce every spring, through the crashing-in of snow and blossoming trees. This time, half-way through the scrap woods of West Virginia, I read out loud Joyce's description of the meal laid out at the Misses Morkans' winter party, attended by all their friends and family, including the main character of the story, Gabriel Conroy. The passage reads like a still life painting, burgeoning but balanced, inflorescent with beveled, faceted glass, glistening with sauces and lipids and fruits:

"A fat brown goose lay at one end of the table and at the other end, on a bed of creased paper strewn with sprigs of parsley, lay a great ham, stripped of its outer skin and peppered over with crust crumbs, a neat paper frill round its shin and beside this was a round of spiced beef. Between these rival ends ran parallel lines of side-dishes: two little minsters of jelly, red and yellow; a shallow dish full of blocks of blancmange and red jam, a large green leaf-shaped dish with a stalk-shaped handle, on which lay bunches of purple raisins and peeled almonds, a companion dish on which lay a solid rectangle of Smyrna figs, a dish of custard topped with grated nutmeg, a small bowl full of chocolates and sweets wrapped in gold and silver papers and a glass vase in which stood some tall celery stalks. In the centre of the table there stood, as sentries to a fruit-stand which upheld a pyramid of oranges and American apples, two squat old-fashioned decanters of cut glass, one containing port and the other dark sherry. On the closed square piano a pudding in a huge yellow dish lay in waiting and behind it were three squads of bottles of stout and ale and minerals, drawn up according to the colours of their uniforms, the first two black, with brown and red labels, the third and smallest squad white, with transverse green sashes."

I feel that I might be able trace back to still life painting the reason I convinced K to accompany me to Pittsburgh to see Leibniz's cipher machine in the Hillman Library. In a still life, paper frill, decanter, and apple are compositional, arranged in shapely harmony. Lines and groupings scaffold the chaos of a cornucopia. I love to look at pyramids of oranges and American apples, and hunger, and be filled, not with food, but with forms: fruits assembled in the shape of an inscrutable tomb.

Though he never said so explicitly, Leibniz understood the world in aesthetic terms. Frederick Beiser shows how Leibniz's "view of the world as a work of art or organism" emerges out of his metaphysics, where substance is "the basic unit of reality." According to Leibniz, substance is a "living force…with the power to unify a manifold, to create unity amid variety." As Beiser reminds us, "Unity amid variety is order or harmony, which is the structure of beauty itself." Substance, then, which is unity, expresses itself as beauty.

Ours, then, less a world of apples, than of pyramids.

In Pittsburgh, through intermittent, furious snow-showers that disperse as soon into late sunlight, K and I walk among the graves at Homewood Cemetery near Frick Park. As snow begins to fall again, we spot deer among the headstones, observing, too, several marble crypts with columns interspersed, and the absurd pyramid that looms through the mist on the hilltop and marks the final resting place of William Harry Brown, banker and heir to a shipping empire. It snows faster, hard and blindingly, at an angle, and we are obliged to turn and walk backwards against the white force, backwards through a graveyard. Our reversal of the right way of things, I worry, might be the start of some summoning, an incantation without intent. So I turn back to face my blindness, and K laughs that there are snowflakes in my eyelashes.

Beiser reports on Leibniz, who believed "even sensual or physical pleasure is aesthetic…because it derives from the perception of a perfection, even if we are not fully aware of the perfection itself." In other words, as Leibniz put it in a letter to Sophia Charlotte, a queen and daughter of the house of Brunswick-Lüneburg, the sensual world is, in its essence, occult, the reason for our feelings hidden from us.

Nicholas Rescher, the philosophy professor at Pittsburgh who built Leibniz's cipher machine for the first time in 2011, writes that Leibniz designed his device to be portable, "readily contained in a box sufficiently small to escape notice among the impedimenta of a travelling prince."

En route to Pittsburgh, I glimpse from the freeway a cluster of shipping containers sloped on a hillside. A billboard with the words "American Homes" hovers nearby.

At first, Leibniz was interested in cryptography not because he wanted to hide his thoughts from others, but because he saw it as kin to algebra, part of the general science of human knowledge. His early writings on cryptography show that he hoped that theory, or rather a clear, methodological set of rules, could be applied to the art of decryption. In fact, Leibniz viewed the whole scientific method in cryptologic terms. To him, a hypothesis was "like the key to a cryptograph, and the simpler it [was], and the greater the number of events that [could] be explained by it, the more probable it [was]." But he also understood that, just as a complex cipher can be solved using multiple keys, with only one revealing the true message, a hypothesis can never be proven beyond doubt, since "the same effects can have several causes."

Furthermore, Leibniz saw the world as an encrypted text. To obtain scientific knowledge about it is like solving a cipher. But the philosopher's skeptical ideas about science and hypotheses meant that it was entirely possible to find a bad key that still made sense.

It is possible to think you have found it, but you haven't—it retreats into the woods. You may never know, thinking you do. You may never feast, though you feel your belly full. The Heinz Memorial Chapel aspires behind the massive, gothic high rise of the Cathedral of Learning, where the ninety-year-old Rescher keeps his offices. The Heinz Chapel has 4,000 square feet of stained glass. Each of its 23 windows, some of which ascend to a height of 73 feet, depict famous authors, scientists, and theologians, representing men and women equally. One page of an "Alphabetical List of the Figures in the Windows" reports the installment in glass of Galileo, Gamaliel, Saint Genevieve, Christopher Gist, and God. Gist is described as an "American frontiersmen." God is described as "divinity of the three great monotheistic religions."

Just as much a part.

Emily Dickinson is here, too. In an aureole of red shards, Dickinson holds a fascicle and a quill. The parchment reads: "A wounded deer leaps highest." Above her head leaps a stag. At her feet is a snake—"a narrow fellow in the grass"—and a mourning dove—"a bird came down the walk."

The summer before K and I met each other while studying literature at the University of North Carolina, we had both attended an academic conference in Paris focused on Emily Dickinson. It's possible we sat together in the same room, not knowing that one day we would stand together in the Heinz Memorial Chapel, two cognoscenti looking up at Dickinson in glass while chapel stewards indulged their visitors by playing bits from Bach's "The Art of the Fugue" overhead on the great pipe organ. That summer, in the days leading up to the conference, I wandered Paris and its suburbs trying to make sense of the recent stadium bombing and shooting at the Bataclan club. At the time of my visit to the Stade de France in Saint Denis, I didn't know the suburb had one of the highest recruitment rates in Europe for ISIS. I didn't know that some of the terrorists responsible for the attack had been killed in Saint Denis, in a shoot-out with the police less than two miles from the ancient basilica where all the kings of France are buried. The night I learned these things I couldn't sleep. My heart leapt and leapt in my chest, constricting my breath.

It was hard for me to locate the source of my panic. In retrospect, part of me thinks my response was fear, the fear of having been close to death without knowing it.

Another part of me knows I was thrilled to panic, too. Not the perverse, sadistic thrill of having witnessed someone else's violence, but, more perversely, the thrill of making connections, synthesizing a network of underground associations. The thrill of being included in a vast plot stretching from Syria to Saint Denis, all the way from Clovis I to Emily Dickinson to the Eagles of Death Metal.

But if the world is encrypted, who is its cryptographer? And why? What is there to hide?

I learn from Leibniz that, when it comes to cryptographic discovery, analysis is not enough: instead, in the non-methodological, "rambling hunt (*vaga venatio*)" of decryption, "a more extensive (*longior*) procedure of synthesis will prove necessary."

But accurate decryption depends on a finite text—one not too long, not too short. When the text is limited, Rescher writes, "a meaningful decoding is its own verification." On the other hand, when the text is nature, as Leibniz believed, and nature's text is limitless, "our 'decryptions' thereof afford no more than the moral certainty of high probability." No higher than a hunted deer. And I am the deer here. And I am the shooter.

Perhaps the lesson of the Fall is a lesson in cryptography. Taste of the fruit of knowledge and be buried. Be encrypted. Underneath a pyramid of apples.

Leibniz's cipher machine is modeled after his calculator, an ornate system of gears and screws arranged around a "stepped drum," called a *staffelwalze*. This "Leibniz-wheel" is engineered so that it can mesh variably with other, more regularly shaped and rotating gears. Each drum has six "steps" that are designed to either lock with or skip the teeth of the other gears. The result is that the rotation sequence of the machine can be programmed depending on the user. In his calculator, the *staffelwalze* permits a carrying operation and multiple mathematic functions. In his cipher machine, the *staffelwalze* allows for increasingly complex and variable cryptographic permutations.

On first seeing the stepped drum, K says it looks like a nautilus shell.

In the Hillman Library, we are shown the machine and how it works, and provided access to a handful of other papers by or about Leibniz, including a handwritten letter he addressed in 1711 to Michael Gottlieb Hansch, a Kepler scholar. The letter treats the topics of the Fall, infant sin, free will, liberty, perception, and, in passing, Hansch's work on an edition of Johannes Kepler's writing.

The cipher machine is designed to be used as one might play a harpsichord. Leibniz returns to this analogue repeatedly in his letters: "While both encipherment and decipherment is [ordinarily] laborious, there is now a facility enabling one to get at the requisite ciphers or alphabetic-letters as easily as though one were playing on a clavichord or other [keyboard] instrument." The special collections librarian explains to us that, because the device was built for demonstration purposes, their version doesn't include the decode function, which would involve the installment of some extra parts. Thus, the first of only two existing versions of Leibniz's celebrated cipher machine can only be used to encrypt messages. The only song you can play is a darkening song.

Around the time of the machine's construction, Nicholas Rescher donated Leibniz's letter to Hansch to the Hillman Library. In the letter, Leibniz refutes Spinoza and Descartes's claim that liberty (free will) requires "complete indetermination." To make his point, Leibniz cites Bayle, who said that if "I do not perceive it, hence it is not there." What Leibniz means to say is that if free will exists, it must be determinate in order to be perceptible. That being said, he grants that "even if we do not perceive reasons of necessity, they can certainly still be there. We do not even perceive all of the things actually within us, for we have many confused perceptions whose constituents are not perceived by us." What is perceived is real, but we can't perceive everything. We can't, because we are essentially constrained, essentially confused.

But it is not only that perception is limited. Perception itself cannot be perceived, and so it remains unknowable. I can't touch my touching. I can't see my seeing. The very tool I use to decipher nature's texts is a mechanism that I cannot rationalize or explain to myself. Leibniz illustrates his point by comparing perception to a windmill:

> "One is obliged to admit that perception [i.e. mental activity] and what depends upon it is inexplicable on mechanical principles, that is, by figures and motions. In imagining that there is a machine whose construction would enable it to think, to sense, and to have perception, one could conceive it enlarged while retaining the same proportions, so that one could enter into it, just like into a windmill. Supposing this, one should, when visiting within it, find only parts pushing one another, and never anything by which to explain a perception."

Leibniz enters the windmill of the mind and finds a complexity exceeding the sum of component parts. It cannot be analyzed to be known. Likewise, in his investigation into cryptography, Leibniz gradually realized that codebreaking "is not subject to definite rules (*certis regulis*) but is a matter of ad hoc contrivances whose complexity is ever in the increase."

To know the mind, then—to perceive perception—is to play a complex, ad hoc song that darkens the mind and can't be undone.

I can't decrypt before I encrypt first.

In a study of the mathematical architecture of Bach's "The Art of the Fugue," Loïc Sylvestre and Marco Costa observe that Bach probably read both Johannes Kepler's *Harmonices mundi* (1619) and Mersenne's *Harmonie universelle* (1636), "which gives clear instructions on the use of the geometrical proportion associated with the golden ratio in discussing tuning systems and instrument making." The golden ratio was a subject of lifelong fascination for Kepler, who "in a private letter to Joachim Tanckius dated 12 May 1608, ... explained how he found the numerical expression of F from the Fibonacci sequence." Kepler later published his findings publicly in an essay on the geometric proportions of snowflakes.

Walking snowblind among the indeterminate crypts and pyramids of Pittsburgh, I realize all at once where I am. I realize what Rilke realized, too, that "where you are, there arises a place."

As an ocean rises. A tidal ground.

K laughs that there are nautilus shells on my eyelashes.

According to Emerson, it is not an ocean we walk on, but "molten lava."

His biographer Robert Richardson explains that Emerson came to feel this way after the death of his wife, Ellen, in the winter of 1831. Over a year later, no longer "sure what he really believed, who he really was, or what he should be doing," Emerson still "felt the 'vanishing volatile froth of the present' turning into the fixed adamantine past." Perhaps to return to the froth of the present, to break through the hardening crust of the adamantine past on which walked, Emerson exhumed the corpse of his dead wife with his own hands on March 29, 1832.

Calling this act "essential Emerson," Richardson speculates that Emerson dug up Ellen because "he had a powerful craving for direct, personal, unmediated experience. That is what he meant when he insisted that one should strive for an original relation to the universe. Not a novel relation, just one's own."

In a poem called "Woodnotes," Emerson describes the sense of his "original relation to the universe" as an occult and "fatal song." He invites his reader to learn the same song:

"Come learn with me the fatal song
Which knits the world in music strong;
Come lift thine eyes to lofty rhymes,
Of things with things, of times with times,
Primal chimes of sun and shade,
Of sound and echo, man and maid,

The land reflected in the flood,
Body with shadow still pursued.
For Nature beats in perfect tune,
And rounds with rhyme her every rune,
Whether she work in land or sea,
Or hide underground her alchemy.
Thou canst not wave thy staff in air,
Or dip thy paddle in the lake,
But it carves the bow of beauty there,
And the ripples in rhymes the oar forsake."

For Emerson, just living was enough to be in an endless, fated state of singing a fatal song, conjuring beauty from thin air, summoning up from underground she who works in land or sea, in "the land reflected in the flood."

Come learn with me the fatal song.

On our way to Pittsburgh in the predawn, K and I fall to talking about people we have known, how they have changed, or haven't, and the families they've raised. She remembers a boy she knew in grade school who loved to hunt, who still loves it, who, now a grown man, posts snapshots of dead deer to social media on a regular basis. She tells me it disgusts her to see, and she mourns for the creatures her classmate has killed. We talk about our fathers and their guns. Talk turns to her ex, Jacob, when she remembers that after their breakup, he had left his shotgun in her apartment, where it still remained in a closet. She begins to worry out loud about possessing a firearm without a license. We wonder what the procedure is like for surrendering guns to the police. Eventually, the conversation wanders to other subjects. Once it gets light enough to see, somewhere in West Virginia, I begin to read "The Dead" out loud to K.

The poet Robert Browning lies at the heart of "The Dead." Joyce calls Browning's verse a "thought-tormented music." Gabriel worries that the speech he gives at dinner, including a reference to Browning's poems, might go over his audiences' heads. In his speech, Browning's thought-tormented music morphs into the "thought-tormented age" that Gabriel laments as his audience's and his own.

Later, after the party, Gabriel's wife Gretta, overhears another character singing a mournful song called "The Lass of Aughrim." The song causes her to remember a boy she used to know and love in Galway. The seventeen-year-old boy, named Michael Furey, died as he and Gretta were only beginning to fall in love. To his bewilderment, Gabriel learns that his wife has harbored this young lover in her heart for years. Brought to light by a song overheard by his wife behind a closed door, this new knowledge estranges Gabriel both from Gretta and from himself. Back at their rented room, after Gretta has told the story of Michael Furey to Gabriel and fallen to sleep, Joyce writes that a stunned, stupefied Gabriel

> "…stretched himself cautiously along under the sheets and lay down beside his wife. One by one, they were all becoming shades. Better pass boldly into that other world, in the full glory of some passion, than fade and wither dismally with age. He thought of how she who lay beside him had locked in her heart for so many years that image of her lover's eyes when he had told her that he did not wish to live…. [I]n the partial darkness he imagined he saw the form of a young man standing under a dripping tree. Other forms were near. His soul had approached that region where dwell the vast hosts of the dead. He was conscious of, but could not apprehend, their wayward and flickering existence. His own identity was fading out into a grey impalpable world: the solid world itself, which these dead had one time reared and lived in, was dissolving and dwindling."

When we return home from Pittsburgh the next day, K begins to obsess about the shotgun in her closet. She says she can't stand that it's there. At dinner, she searches her phone for a way to get rid of it. She worries out loud that she could be arrested for hiding a gun that isn't hers. Should she throw it away? Into a dumpster? A river? Increasingly distraught, she asks me to hold her. I do. The following day, she asks me to accompany her to the police station, where dispatch sends an officer to collect the gun at her apartment. They check if it's loaded in the living room.

Later, K's therapist speculates that the reason she couldn't stand, suddenly, to have Jacob's gun in her home is because it represented a threat to her identity. A threat that had been there, with her, repressed, for nearly a year—then all at once exhumed on the road to Pittsburgh, passing the motels and motel pools of Winston-Salem, remembering, like some distant fatal song, a boy she used to know. Who she still follows. Who still follows her.

Song sings to song: the ground opens up.

To decrypt himself (his self a sound and echo of a fatal song), Emerson decrypts his dead wife.

When he realizes his wife's insoluble encryption, the dead boy buried in her heart, Gabriel becomes encrypted to himself and to the world and the world is entombed in snow. The song she heard was fatal to them both, stirring up Furey like dust in her heart.

What I do to myself I can't do without you.

(What I do to myself I do to you.)

The song of myself, I sing it to you.

(Song of myself I can't sing without you.)

Before I go, the librarian allows me to press a single letter on the keyboard of Leibniz's cipher machine. Remembering the inscriptions on the Temple of Delphi, among them the three Delphic maxims ("know thyself," "nothing in excess," and "make a pledge and mischief is nigh") plus a large, cryptic letter E, I choose to play the letter E.

Coda

Here breaches the whale:

On display for a time at the Denver Art Museum was a graphite print by Justin Quinn called *Moby Dick Chapter 44 or 4206 times E* (2005).

The print comprises only iterations, over and over, of the letter E, concatenated to form lengthy, monotonous, roping chains that loop around the border and coil inward. That column and snake. That paragraph and break. The work cuts all but the letter E out of a transcription of Chapter 44 of *Moby-Dick*, "The Chart."

In this chapter, Captain Ahab reads nautical charts in his cabin, plotting out his wild trajectory through all the oceans of the earth in search of his sole desire, the white whale. As Melville describes it, the lines that Ahab marks on the map are copied onto his forehead, too, so that his focus is also the paradigm of his pursuit:

> "[W]hile he himself was marking out lines and courses on the wrinkled charts, some invisible pencil was also tracing lines and courses upon the deeply marked chart of his forehead... [W]ith the charts of all four oceans before him, Ahab was threading a maze of currents and eddies, with a view to the more certain accomplishment of that monomaniac thought of his soul."

When asked, why E, Quinn responds that he was struck by the Snellen chart, used for testing visual acuity. Each chart has, of course, at the apex of a pyramid of diminishing letters, a large, beaconing E.

For Quinn, the mark of clarity becomes the sign of obsession.

When I look at *Moby Dick Chapter 44 or 4206 times E,* I don't read it as E and E and E and E and so on, nor as a shape, nor a design.

I read it, instead, as a scream.

EEEEEEEEEEEEEEEEEEEEEEEEEEEEEEEEEEEEEEEEEEEEEEEEEEE
EEEEEEEEEEEEEEEEEEEEEEEEEEEEEEEEEEEEEEEEEEEEEEEEEEE
EEEEEEEEEEEEEEEEEEEEEEEEEEEEEEEEEEEEEEEEEEEEEEEEEEE

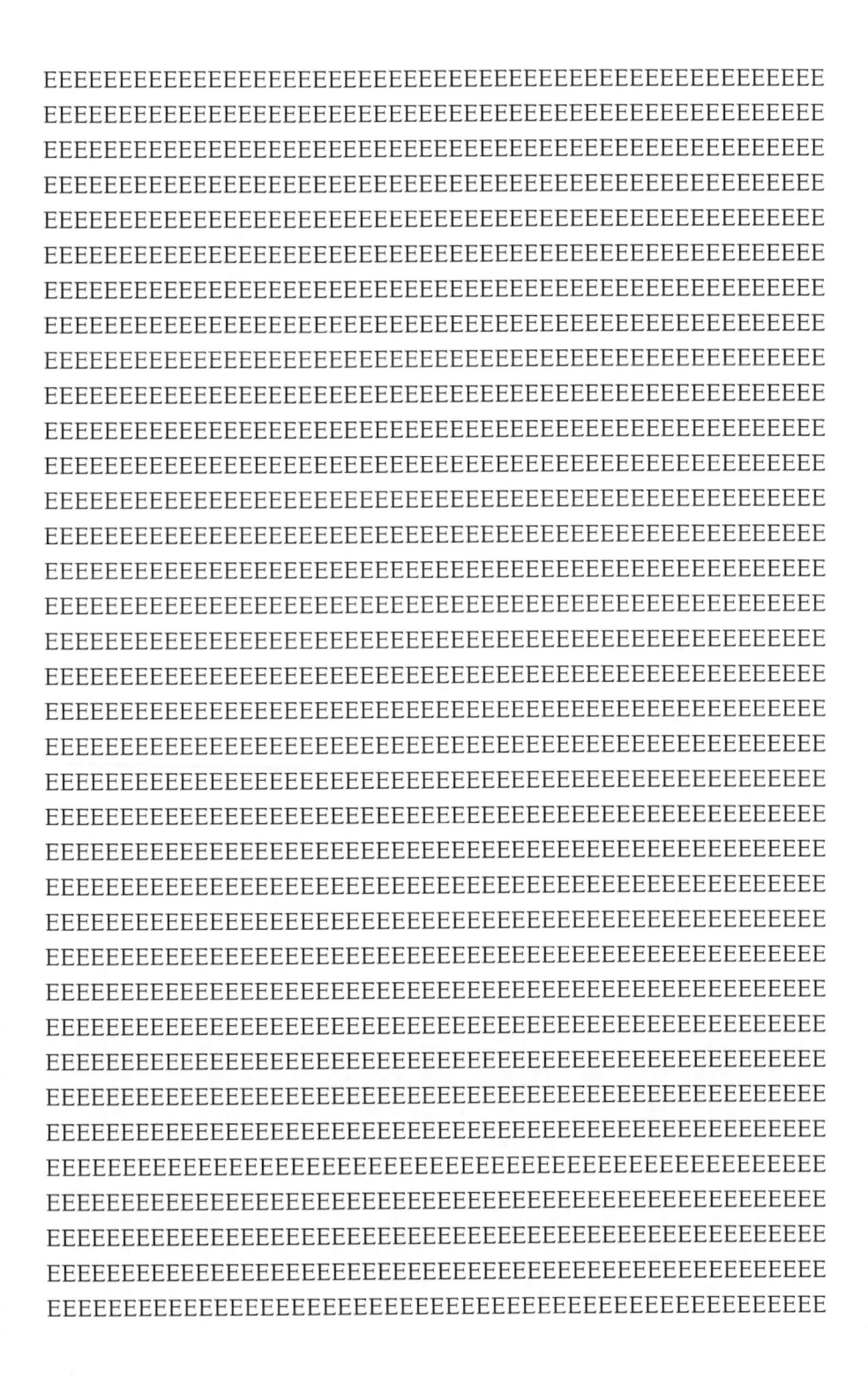

EEEEEEEEEEEEEEEEEEEEEEEEEEEEEEEEEEEEEEEEEEEEEEEEEEEE
EEEEEEEEEEEEEEEEEEEEEEEEEEEEEEEEEEEEEEEEEEEEEEEEEEEE
EEEEEEEEEEEEEEEEEEEEEEEEEEEEEEEEEEEEEEEEEEEEEEEEEEEE
EEEEEEEEEEEEEEEEEEEEEEEEEEEEEEEEEEEEEEEEEEEEEEEEEEEE
EEEEEEEEEEEEEEEEEEEEEEEEEEEEEEEEEEEEEEEEEEEEEEEEEEEE
EEEEEEEEEEEEEEEEEEEEEEEEEEEEEEEEEEEEEEEEEEEEEEEEEEEE
EEEEEEEEEEEEEEEEEEEEEEEEEEEEEEEEEEEEEEEEEEEEEEEEEEEE
EEEEEEEEEEEEEEEEEEEEEEEEEEEEEEEEEEEEEEEEEEEEEEEEEEEE
EEEEEEEEEEEEEEEEEEEEEEEEEEEEEEEEEEEEEEEEEEEEEEEEEEEE
EEEEEEEEEEEEEEEEEEEEEEEEEEEEEEEEEEEEEEEEEEEEEEEEEEEE
EEEEEEEEEEEEEEEEEEEEEEEEEEEEEEEEEEEEEEEEEEEEEEEEEEEE
EEEEEEEEEEEEEEEEEEEEEEEEEEEEEEEEEEEEEEEEEEEEEEEEEEEE
EEEEEEEEEEEEEEEEEEEEEEEEEEEEEEEEEEEEEEEEEEEEEEEEEEEE
EEEEEEEEEEEEEEEEEEEEEEEEEEEEEEEEEEEEEEEEEEEEEEEEEEEE
EEEEEEEEEEEEEEEEEEEEEEEEEEEEEEEEEEEEEEEEEEEEEEEEEEEE
EEEEEEEEEEEEEEEEEEEEEEEEEEEEEEEEEEEEEEEEEEEEEEEEEEEE
EEEEEEEEEEEEEEEEEEEEEEEEEEEEEEEEEEEEEEEEEEEEEEEEEEEE
EEEEEEEEEEEEEEEEEEEEEEEEEEEEEEEEEEEEEEEEEEEEEEEEEEEE
EEEEEEEEEEEEEEEEEEEEEEEEEEEEEEEEEEEEEEEEEEEEEEEEEEEE
EEEEEEEEEEEEEEEEEEEEEEEEEEEEEEEEEEEEEEEEEEEEEEEEEEEE
EEEEEEEEEEEEEEEEEEEEEEEEEEEEEEEEEEEEEEEEEEEEEEEEEEEE
EEEEEEEEEEEEEEEEEEEEEEEEEEEEEEEEEEEEEEEEEEEEEEEEEEEE
EEEEEEEEEEEEEEEEEEEEEEEEEEEEEEEEEEEEEEEEEEEEEEEEEEEE
EEEEEEEEEEEEEEEEEEEEEEEEEEEEEEEEEEEEEEEEEEEEEEEEEEEE
EEEEEEEEEEEEEEEEEEEEEEEEEEEEEEEEEEEEEEEEEEEEEEEEEEEE
EEEEEEEEEEEEEEEEEEEEEEEEEEEEEEEEEEEEEEEEEEEEEEEEEEEE
EEEEEEEEEEEEEEEEEEEEEEEEEEEEEEEEEEEEEEEEEEEEEEEEEEEE
EEEEEEEEEEEEEEEEEEEEEEEEEEEEEEEEEEEEEEEEEEEEEEEEEEEE
EEEEEEEEEEEEEEEEEEEEEEEEEEEEEEEEEEEEEEEEEEEEEEEEEEEE
EEEEEEEEEEEEEEEEEEEEEEEEEEEEEEEEEEEEEEEEEEEEEEEEEEEE
EEEEEEEEEEEEEEEEEEEEEEEEEEEEEEEEEEEEEEEEEEEEEEEEEEEE
EEEEEEEEEEEEEEEEEEEEEEEEEEEEEEEEEEEEEEEEEEEEEEEEEEEE
EEEEEEEEEEEEEEEEEEEEEEEEEEEEEEEEEEEEEEEEEEEEEEEEEEEE
EEEEEEEEEEEEEEEEEEEEEEEEEEEEEEEEEEEEEEEEEEEEEEEEEEEE
EEEEEEEEEEEEEEEEEEEEEEEEEEEEEEEEEEEEEEEEEEEEEEEEEEEE
EEEEEEEEEEEEEEEEEEEEEEEEEEEEEEEEEEEEEEEEEEEEEEEEEEEE
EEEEEEEEEEEEEEEEEEEEEEEEEEEEEEEEEEEEEEEEEEEEEEEEEEEE

EEEEEEEEEEEEEEEEEEEEEEEEEEEEEEEEEEEEEEEEEEEEEEEEEEEE
EEEEEEEEEEEEEEEEEEEEEEEEEEEEEEEEEEEEEEEEEEEEEEEEEEEE
EEEEEEEEEEEEEEEEEEEEEEEEEEEEEEEEEEEEEEEEEEEEEEEEEEEE
EEEEEEEEEEEEEEEEEEEEEEEEEEEEEEEEEEEEEEEEEEEEEEEEEEEE
EEEEEEEEEEEEEEEEEEEEEEEEEEEEEEEEEEEEEEEEEEEEEEEEEEEE
EEEEEEEEEEEEEEEEEEEEEEEEEEEEEEEEEEEEEEEEEEEEEEEE

Bees

Many of my friends are poets. Images from their poems hang in a room in my head. N, whose image is the brown light of a library on a hill in New Jersey, tells me that mine is a tent-flap unzipped in the middle of the woods. On a separate occasion, without consulting N, my friend H (whose image is a crystal held in a mouth) confirms this is my truest image: what it is like to emerge at dawn from a dewy, collapsible structure at the end of the world.

Images from my friend C's poems take up perhaps the most head-space. We wrote and lived together as college roommates in a town of chapels and temples in the intermountain west. When I think about him now, I picture a moth in a paper bag. From poem to poem, the image wandered as he revised: sometimes the paper bag was a cathedral, other times a heart. Always with a battered moth in it.

Years after graduating and moving away from each other, C and I meet in Las Vegas, in February. I am in town for an academic conference at the university to talk about Leibniz and poetry. Vegas is C's hometown, though these days he lives with his wife in Santa Cruz, where he works on a novel. His father lives alone in a house full of books on theology in Summerlin, twenty minutes from the strip, where he practices law as a defense attorney. A devout Mormon, the reason he stays in Vegas is church. My friend jokes that his dad has built up a reputation as a local scholiast; church members consult him often with esoteric questions on scripture.

I like Vegas for the same reason most people do. You go to lose something. C takes me drinking on the strip before lunch. A buddy of his from high school tends the bar at a new sushi restaurant next to the Golden Knights stadium. Ice hockey in the desert. Lunch is red fish roe and sake bombs. I feel drunk when I check in to the conference on the university campus later that afternoon.

At the beginning of the eighteenth century, Leibniz wrote that "nothing is fallow, sterile, or dead in the universe." Indeed, "every bit of matter can be conceived as a garden full of plants or a pond full of fish. But each branch of the plant, each member of the animal, each drop of its bodily fluids, is also such a garden or such a pond." All matter is fractal, then. A single instance of life is inclusive of all life. In one of his essays, Emerson wrote that "[t]he creation of a thousand forests is in one acorn, and Egypt, Greece, Rome, Gaul, Britain, America, lie folded already in the first man." History is the process of unfolding what is already there. Emerson uses this logic to suggest that the meanest biographical detail is a true expression of all the temples and economies and engines of war that have preceded and inflect a life.

He says: you were always supposed to be here. You and everything else.

Nothing is fallow and sterile. Anything is a pond full of fish. This goes for the fragile artifice of Vegas. Every hour, the Bellagio fountains throw water from Lake Mead into the sky. Most of Lake Mead, the largest reservoir in the United States and source of much of the city's water, derives from the Colorado River, passed through an intricate system of dams and diversions. To account for water shortages, lawmakers have improvised a labyrinth of regulations, spillways, and washes to respond to periods of flash flooding as well as drought. Since the land is unretentive sand and rock, miles of flood tunnels twist underground. In the midst of these intricacies, you start to forget the meadows that first gave the city its Spanish name. Today the artesian aquifers are dry. A city shivers there instead, permanent mirage.

After the conference, my flight home is a red-eye. Since C has plans already to see the Knights, his dad drives me to the airport, not far from the strip. While we skim through the dark, we talk about the nature of God and Christ. To be able to participate in the conversation, I muster a muffled religious sensibility to say that I like to think of God as mysterious, distant, rather than personal, paternal, Protestant. My friend's dad listens carefully, and then explains why he believes the opposite. He loves a God who loves, and who shows it through grace. To illustrate his point, he tells the story of a family on a road trip: A father's young son realizes he has forgotten a favorite toy car back home. The boy is inconsolable. Irritated at first, the father decides to turn back home to find the toy, even though their trip by now is well under way. As he tells this small story, C's father struggles to keep emotion out of his voice. Distracted, he misses the airport exit and we have to loop again around the beltway. God is the same way with us, he says. Always turning back.

An image is like a story. It is what you picture when you think about your life, or when you talk about God. C invited me to be best man at his wedding. When it was time for me to give a speech, I shared an anecdote about his favorite poet, Donald Revell. When Revell tells his story, he calls it "the only experience" he has ever had—an image of paradise to which he returns again and again when writing his poems:

> "When I was a boy, my father drove us once very fast along a road deep in a woodland. The leaves on the trees turned into mirrors, signaling with bright lights frantically. They said it was the end of the world and to go faster. We were in the Catskills. Suddenly the road ahead and the woods around us turned brilliant, pure white—but not blinding. My father kept driving. There were no cars but ours. After a while, my mother and sister and I began to chatter, at first frantically, but then delightedly, about how beautiful the white forest and all the white leaves and how perfect the pine needles were. It was clear to all of us, though none of us said so, that we had died, and were motoring through heaven. Having no need to slow down, my father drove faster and faster. After a few minutes, the trees were just as suddenly green again, and the two-lane asphalt top, black. We got home fine, and had our supper."

When I told the story of this image at my friend's wedding, I think I was trying to say something about family and delight. And how people see each other by seeing visions. When I first wrote about that tent in the woods in a poem, what I didn't describe to my friends is that, in the image, my father, mother, brother and sister are all there sleeping warmly in bags behind me. Later on, we decamp, pack the car, get home fine, and have our supper. It is like nothing ever happened. But the image remains.

I read once, in a book written by a former teacher of mine, a description of silver poplar leaves, seen from inside mid-summer, late afternoon. I don't know why I remember this detail in particular, but when I close my eyes and try to think of a way to write about what it's like to look at an after-image on a sunny day in a dark room, I imagine my teacher's tree, hiving in light, every leaf the edge of a brimming cell, the effect in all a flashing swarm of microsaccades, or the tiny movements of the eye as it adjusts itself to over-stimulus, as it shifts the imprint elsewhere on the retina.

If I look away, I can carry the drifting burning picture into my dim interior. I can glance across the bookshelf along the opposite dark wall, and see a tree, fading fast, now in negative, flashed there by the photochemical cascade still going on inside me.

Looking long enough to see anything involves a loss of sensitivity. I am blinded for a moment by the outline of an image I can only see because what I saw before was too much to process without searing it into me. When the eye builds an image on the retina that lasts when I look away, it is a structure of damage whose repair is also its dismantling, a razing to the basement crypts.

When I move across the country, I carry a way of looking at one landscape to another, still blinded by the gas and grasslands of the high plains west, by the afterimages of silos, frack sites, the irrigation ditches that drive water from the mountains into dry plains. Leaving Colorado, I try looking with similar eyes at the Carolina piedmonts, at its gutted textile mills and eroded farms and idle towns, flush with greenery. I try looking for a way in, a way to understand a place as its thickness in time, its ruins, and what has sedimented over them.

One way in, I have read, is the image. The poet Marianne Boruch writes: "There is the thinnest veil between the things we see and the secret, heart-stopping place those images open to, and only image, the beloved particular, allows entry."

Or maybe I am just looking for a way to see—here, too—something where nothing is.

A dinner guest one summer night, I ask some new friends if they use the pond on their five-acre plot to irrigate. They laugh and remind me that I don't live out west anymore. I have moved to a place where things just green and fill with bees. No need for the mazy systems of pipe and sluicegate, deferral and diversion to which I had grown accustomed in high, dry homes like Colorado or Nevada.

It is then I recognize that the movement of water from Point A to Point B has long been for me a means to see a place, to study the ditches of desire cutting through it. To remember the flood-trenches I dug around my home as a boy beside my father. To remember Xerxes at the Hellespont whipping the Aegean with a chain when it didn't calm the way he wanted, ripping through his bridges instead.

There is plenty here already. I blink and strain. The overbrightness starts to pull apart across my optic nerve. I try to peer through the images I have learned to see. In their place, already the new green and yawing highways that hurl me between sheds and mills and dams are burning into me the lines of a city whose basic building block is light. Sight is a boomtown: I build and build like it's nothing, then move on, abandon it to grass, do it all again. And for the smallest, most focused moment, I lived a life in that place. The friends I grew to love, then left there—I carry their images with me. I save these first as the burning walls of my sight burn down again, flinging them in their frames from a window to the black lawn below, my gaze flickering fly-like from the surging surfaces of screen to desk to beveled glass to silver tree.

In a book about the sea, Lebanese-American poet and artist Etel Adnan writes, "Behind an image there's the image." Elsewhere, Adnan clarifies that what she means is that an image involves more than what it pictures. The whole of the world upholds it.

Without walls to hang from and interiors to fill, painting as we know it couldn't have developed. A painting is always supported by an infrastructure, material as well as pictorial. Perhaps this is most true of the *trompe l'oeil*, in which the painter tries to pass her image off as an object among others, inconspicuous hunting gear hanging from a nail against a wooden door. A *vide poche* full of letters and combs and ribbons. A meticulous fly on a frame that turns out to be part of the picture plane. The illusion, or delusion, as some have described it, cannot succeed without assuming that the painting participates as something other than a painting in the room that it occupies. If I look at a *trompe l'oeil* outside the context it implies, the image brings to mind the walls that would otherwise surround it.

Other times it brings in birds. In an anecdote by Pliny the Elder, the ancient Greek painter Zeuxis depicted grapes so convincingly in a painting contest with a rival artist named Parrhasius, that starlings descended to partake and broke their beaks against the glistening still-life surface of the wall.

The painted grapes were a clear success. Exultant, Zeuxis and a gathering crowd turned to Parrhasius and invited him to display his own work, concealed behind a curtain. Parrhasius quietly responded that it couldn't be done. Impatient in the hot sun, Zeuxis pressed his competitor to draw back the curtain, and when Parrhasius again insisted that this was impossible, Zeuxis rushed forward and tried to tear aside the drape, only to discover that this drab scrap of fabric was itself the painting on the wall, a perfect illusion. Though Zeuxis's grapes had summoned birds, Parrhasius was declared the obvious winner, having seduced a human gaze. Later, Pliny reports, the victor gained renown depicting the depths and projective dimensions of bodies. Parrhasius's great distinction was to develop a rounding, receding surface so "as to suggest the presence of other parts behind it also, and disclose even what it hides."

The illusion of the painted curtain depends on its viewer's desire to see what lies behind it. It works only underneath the rough grope of expectation, the mind already pulling it aside, materializing the vague shape of something that doesn't exist behind it, not yet realizing that the painting is an image of my own hunger, my hand scraped raw against a stone wall.

There is nothing else to see here.

It is all already here.

More and more I wonder which is worse: a life of false images, or a life with none at all.

An image is always an afterimage. Even when I look away, it hovers before me, building my sight.

As an experiment, I remove all the images and icons from my walls, all the photos in my wallet, all the mementos and souvenirs on my shelves, and set my desktop a white screen. It is as if I'm burning them, iconoclast like Emerson, who focused not on the image but on the eye, what unifies. It is the I's eye that aggregates and so perceives: "There is a property in the horizon which no man has but he whose eye can integrate all the parts." This "axis of vision" is "coincident with the axis of things." The world is your sight. When you look at the world, you see your sight, and vice versa. Seeing yourself seeing is everything: "Not in nature but in man is all the beauty and worth he sees. The world is very empty, and is indebted to this gilding, exalting soul for all its pride."

Emerson teaches that when you see yourself see you can catch a glimpse of your own original relation to the universe, unmediated by the distracting images or usages of others.

What I'm going for, I guess, is a bare wall, a structureless eye. I want to look at looking, turn my eye upon itself, peer down both ends of the telescope, and so see the world.

But now I find that, without images surrounding me, I can't see anything.

I am left, even more so than before, with only a blind desire to see. There is my desire, my bleeding parting fingertips, there is a wall. For every wall, there is a city of walls. There is a city far from the sea supported by a distant watershed. There is a father who isn't mine who drives me to the airport in the middle of the night. In the story about God that he tells me, there is a toy car, and in the toy car there is a family, motoring through heaven down a corridor of shining silver leaves.

Behind an image, there is the desire that I see it with. It is desire, desire for the beloved particular, that allows me entry. I push aside the image like a veil, curtain, or a tent-flap.

Or, no: behind the image is whatever is in front of me.

It is from the image that I awake. Zipper of a tent in the middle of the woods. So here we are, so far away from home.

On my hands and knees beneath an archway of fiberglass, bent poles, stakes in the dirt.

Condensation on the polyester flaps. Diaphanous, self-dismantling.

In addition to her poetry and prose, Etel Adnan makes paintings. She makes fold-out accordion books called *leporellos,* whose panels of Japanese paper feature fragments of text and color and figure. One of her painted books contains a series of poems in Arabic. Because Adnan does not normally compose in Arabic, some have observed that the writing takes on the appearance of pictures: Joana Hadjithomas and Khalil Joreige write that "her gestures inhabit a language that becomes drawing, like a re-created language that nevertheless refers to an exile within one's territory and, beyond, to a deep interior exile."

I build and then I leave. Collapsible tabernacle.

In ancient Greek, the word used to refer to the human "I" was *hypokeimenon,* which means that which underlies. It did not signify self-reference, it does not point back to itself through both ends of a telescope. Instead, as Hans-Georg Gadamer indicates, for the Greeks, the idea of subjectivity was logically closest to the concept of matter, substance, or substrate. The "I" is not that which turns to look inward. Instead, it is the ground from which I look out.

The object isn't to see seeing, but to see beyond it. To see from the desire that frames my sight.

The first time I share a whole night's sleep with you, it is in a tent borrowed from some friends, set up beside a wild apple tree in Shenandoah. This time of year, the colors of the leaves, trunk, and yield are all part of the same golden-grey concealment, so it is hard to work out at first in the midst of the changing foliage the subtle knots of old fruit. Pick one, and see its worm-etched surface is the map of a world. The next morning, in the car on the drive back, the rapid light I watch fluting through the trees is like the nights and days of a thousand years at once.

Once I might have said I'm sorry, I should be quiet, I have no place to speak in this abundance. I have no place to say I have no place.

But I know that isn't true.

Because I do. That place is right in front of me; there is nothing else to see. It builds with loss inside my eye the light that crosses the windshield and grazes your jaw. It barely misses you, that arrow, but pierces me and festers, recipe for bees:

Slaughter a bull and place it in the shed in the winter, the Roman poet wrote. By summer you'll have a swarm. It will pollinate your fields that need no watering. Nothing is fallow or dead in the universe.

By bees I mean a hiving tree of silver leaves. By leaves I mean the thousand movements of the eye as it tries to adjust, to see beyond sight, building image after afterimage, city after city, an Egypt, a Greece, a Rome, a Gaul, a Britain, an America—to see beyond sight to the thing that it sees. What is already there. What is right in front of me.

A SIMPLE LIFE

The simplest thing I can think of is a lupin seed. He lives a simple life who eats it, which eating is the smallest giving-in. The lupin seed's uncomplicated status is best preserved in a cool, dry place, away from activating depths like dirt and water.

Diogenes lived the simple life by sleeping seed-like in a storage jar. In his self-imposed poverty the philosopher said: "Everything belongs to the gods; the wise are the friends of the gods; friends hold all things in common; ergo, everything belongs to the wise."

Four of us, all poets in various stages of transition away from poetry, spend a weekday morning at the beach, fully clothed, sipping Stiegl Radlers. W reports he nearly got laid last night after a long conversation with a woman in a bar, but she asked him if he believed in God, and he said he did, or at least in mystery, knowing even as he said it, reluctant to betray his faith, that he had failed her worldly test.

I think I would have said complexity. God, if I believe, is the complex. That is, whatever comes over and above things summed. Take consciousness. Take cities. Take the weather. Like all cosmogonies, or the anarchies and ensuing hierarchies of gods, they stabilize into self-sufficient systems, sun-centered, autopoetic.

But every system has its blindness, or else it wouldn't be one. A hull is how you know you have a seed. An apple has two sides—the side that sweetens in the sun, and whatever side you see. The opposite of what you think resides in shadow does. It's an old idea.

Dressed in rags, Diogenes was questioned who is rich among men. To which he replied, "He who is self-sufficient." He who is a system, internally coherent, or whose complexities have stabilized into a self, that thing extrapolated from a mirror, the sighting of which initiates a blindness. In *Narkissos*, a monumental graphite drawing of a collage by the American artist Jess, the curving, naked body of a young man holding a backscratcher shaped like a hand kneels on the banks of a black pond, its gaping surface filled with lily pads and lilies, floating masks, pentagrams, stars of David. If he gazes at his own face, he only does so through gaps in the reeds and trash, perhaps the spilled contents of a curiosity cabinet, emptied out into a koi pond. Behind the young Narcissus, the strict god Eros, also naked, stands with a bow and an arrow knocked, the barred wings of a falcon extending from his back, his head haloed by a decahedron filled in with a densely penciled geometric pattern, which reminds me of a Pennsylvania Dutch hex sign. Eros is blind, black holes where his eyes should be. A multitude of pasted images constellate and spin around the two naked bodies, a chaotic, campy symposium including a hooded sphinx, a goat-man playing panpipes, tribal totems, swimmers, statuettes, disembodied eyes, an apartment complex, a deep canyon and its river, miniature figures from myth and children's books and comic strips, butterflies, starlings, and peacocks. There is a large dam in the right-hand corner, likely sketched from something snipped from a *National Geographic,* and across its spillway a herd of unshorn sheep are led by their shepherd.

The artist worked on *Narkissos* for fifteen years, from 1976 to 1991. Originally, Jess intended to "translate" his collage of magazine cut-outs into both a pencil drawing as well as, subsequently, a painting. But the image-making never seemed to end, never passed beyond the penciled-in, the erasable stage. One scholar writes that the artist stopped because he "believed he was becoming obsessed with the drawing—that it was expanding more than being completed." What holds the work together as a system, then, its chaos at least internally coherent, is the arbitrary, or rather the completely necessary decision to stop, faced with the possibility of its limitless expansion, the insane eclipse of the life that makes. Framed, the work contains its blindness within it, Love with his eyes missing from his head, a little distant from a self, his self-sufficiency symbolized and sceptered in a backscratcher, who gazes longingly down into a floating pile of trash and thinks he sees his own image, thinking himself a self when really what he is is a growing disarray, restrained, held within a frame solely by the artist's decision to walk away. To call it good, and live.

After he lost his sanity, the poet Hölderlin lived alone in a tower in Tübingen and kept trying to write the poems of pure immanence with which he tasked himself at the height of his intellectual powers. His vocabulary began to dwindle. The poems grew increasingly simple. He signed some of them with a pseudonym—Scardinelli—and dated them erratically. 1648. 1778. 1940. The poems are so simple as to resist interpretation. Their clarity is an index of their irreducibility to meaning: "Still you can see the season, and the field / Of summer shows its mildness and its pride. / The meadow's green is splendidly outspread / Where down the brook and all its wavelets glide."

Of the images in these late poems, one of Hölderlin's biographers writes that "[t]he pictures, the bare phenomena, become an end in themselves and their being realized in poetry is, at one and the same time, all that Hölderlin was capable of and what he had always tried to do."

Your triumph a function of your decline.

Diogenes broke his only cup when he realized he could hold water in his hand long enough to drink from it.

Nature has already equipped me with a cup, he is supposed to have said. Yet Plutarch calls Diogenes' way of life, because self-chosen, "arduous and *un*natural."

On foot, C and I crest a hill of white, sun-fried grass and survey the cardinal points. Below us, the opulent glades of the preserve, a green gemstone of land, fringed by a highway, and set aside as penance for a catastrophic spill in '88. Beyond the wetlands, in the west, the Shell Martinez refinery, a moon city sprawl of orbs, pillars, and towers of intricate scaffolding. In the east, at a greater distance, Tesco Golden Eagle refinery's older-looking superstructure. North, where the Carquinez strait empties into Suisun bay, a small fleet of retired warships. South of us are suburbs, gravel pits.

In the green sedge stilt still, unruffled cranes.

There is a concept at work here, we agree, which is to say an inner tension. But, returning to the preserve's parking lot, we find ourselves content to idle in the shade or shadow of this thought. This feeling of stopping to catch our breath on complexity's temple steps.

It used to be hard for me to love a place like this, its undulations ruined by intrusion, spills and pits. To accept instead the worst of what I have been given, the worst of what we'd made. By "worst" I mean most resistant to conceptualization, meaning hardest to see as more than what it is.

With enough effort, anything can start to feel natural. Everything belongs to the wise, friend of the gods.

I used to think, there must be more. Then, this is all there is. Then, this is enough; this is more than enough. But see how easy it is to spill by accident over into excess. Too much: so kindred to more.

A broken cup filled with loose adhering dandelion seeds is a detail in a photograph by the artist Laura Letinsky, who arranges on white tablecloths sparse still lifes, not painted, but captured on camera.

I used to try to think of what the objects in a still life meant. An unfinished meal, peeled rinds, tipped ewer. The absent human company or appetite. Recent abandonment. Vanity and death. Or, less narratively, what the foodstuff stood for. What brooks the peppered trout, the oysters, the green grapes, all deranged just so. To have sea-meat and land-meat both laid out means temperance, rabbit and lobster a balance of humors. But the still life, too, more essentially, has always been a kind of excuse. A pretext for a play of forms and color and technique. The common objects are simple, available, recognizable and also ripe for endless formal combinations. So it is a lemon faceted by lemon-knife will border on abstraction.

The German philosopher Hegel described the fallacy of an immediate, direct experience of things, or what he called sense-certainty. The idea that there is, before thought, an intuitive grasp of worldly substance. The certainty of something right in front of you, the here-and-now. But, Hegel reminds us, the sense of a here and a now is always changing. Here, for now, is Waterbird Regional Preserve. Now is noon. But here is also, later—or before—a cove on Panther Beach, or a castle at Tübingen.

Now it is night.

Here and now, then, the basic units of sense-certainty, are basest universal categories, general and nonspecific. They can apply anywhere, and to any time.

What was supposed to be the richest source of experience—a direct, intuitive, uncomplicated apprehension of the world—turns out to be the hollowest, most impoverished abstraction.

For Diogenes, finance was the family business; both he and his father were in charge of the state bank and mint. Not yet a philosopher, Diogenes was banished in his youth from Sinope for committing fraud when he restamped the currency. He claimed his exile led him to philosophy.

There are some reports that Diogenes falsified the state currency acting on the advice of the oracle at Delphi, to whom he posed the question: how can I gain the greatest reputation?

Poverty, he taught, teaches us by experience what philosophy teaches by argument: Everything is yours.

A toppled ewer, spilled or drunken to the lees.

Walk quickly enough, and it starts to feel like thinking. With every step a now, a here, collage of them.

Before setting out on foot for food in Chinatown, my former teacher D and I stop at his AirBnB in Greenwich Village to share beers from his fridge. We are both in the city for a scholarly conference on Herman Melville, where we are slated to speak to a bookish audience on what it means to make books out of books—to write of and in the shadow of *Moby-Dick*. He shows me the copy of Diogenes he's been reading.

"When asked what wine he most liked to drink, [the philosopher] replied, 'Somebody else's.'"

The virtues of derivation. Diverting wine from one mouth into another. Courage to be the next to sing.

Loosened by the beer, we walk in the direction of dinner, heads down in the lit dusk, quickened by a deep discussion, not about Melville, but the poet John Keats. His last ode, "To Autumn," which, like Hölderlin's late work, achieves an immanent simplicity, a pure presentation of things as they are. Thereness as ripeness.

"And full-grown lambs loud bleat from hilly bourn; / Hedge-crickets sing; and now with treble soft / The red-breast whistles from a garden-croft; / And gathering swallows twitter in the skies."

Not long after writing "To Autumn," the young poet, in the full thrall of consumption, traveled to Rome to recuperate. Coughing blood and feverish in his hot Roman apartment, he scribbled in the margins of another poem eight short lines:

"This living hand, now warm and capable
Of earnest grasping, would, if it were cold
And in the icy silence of the tomb,
So haunt thy days and chill thy dreaming nights
That thou would wish thine own heart dry of blood
So in my veins red life might stream again,
And thou be conscience-calm'd—see here it is—
I hold it towards you."

The poem, diverting blood from one body, the reader's, into another, the writer's.

These are not the words of someone who has achieved the thoughtless serenity of pure poetic immanence. The pressuring, supplicating "I" so opposes sweet oblivion, the selfless meadows of Autumn's ode.

In the end, in the margins, an anxious, if not irritable, grasping-after.

The poem that follows: the prior poem's failure.

This is enough. This is more than enough. The imperceptible transition from ripe to overripe. From there to too much there. The rind unravels itself. Hundreds of vesicles rupture, their apprehension in the form of taste of citrus also ruins all their granularity: no one cell tasted singly, which is to say specifically.

What can be said specifically? My teacher writes often about the deep virtues of paradox, of saying "I don't know."

But it is sometimes hard to take this seriously. It feels too simple, too easy. A paradox just hangs there, branchless, two-faced apple.

When I tell him so, he suggests that it is harder to achieve not-knowing than I might think. In fact, it is an always unfinished labor. There is, in saying "I don't know," always a margin of knowing that adheres, involved in utterance at all.

Seeds whose lightness is the fringe or bond of their cohesion.

Our neighbors, whose house we watch while they're away, have draped netting across their backyard koi pond, to catch pine needles and keep the hawks from plundering the overstocked waters. It takes up a full third of what was lawn, fed by a rivulet lined with black water-proof plastic. In the dusk, K tosses handfuls of fish food into the pond, whose surface churns into a lemonade of golden bodies. The pond's lily-pad placidity is betrayed by the anxiety that literally shrouds it. The overactive canopy, the predator birds, the absorbent, plastic-bedded dirt. The recirculating brook seems to writhe instead of gently wind.

Of course, koi are kept more for their colors than as a source of tranquility.

This, then, the infrastructure necessary to support an abstraction.

At the Frick with D, Turner's *Cologne, the Arrival of a Packet-Boat: Evening*: A ferry boat filled with female tourists nears the shoreline of the Rhine, browsed by dogs and women hauling timber planks. In the distance, the washed-pink tower of the church of Gross St. Martin. A customs-house. Some battlements. Folded ships at bay. But the focus of the painting is the bright, red-gold refraction of the packing boat's mirror image shattered across the river, in the midst of which a wrecked fishing-trap spiders partway out of the water. The painting's true activity is where figuration warps into a play of light and countercurrent, an ecstatic, dense abstraction. It is as if the commerce and city-building in the scene were there to frame the muscular knot of color and broken form that would come to define Turner's later paintings.

But then you realize the focus is the fish-trap. Remnant of a trade and industry. How it complicates the picture's self-absorption in its inner framed reflections.

Steve has always wanted to take a cruise up the Rhine, to look at castles. But his wife's 99-year-old mother, who lives in her own private suite above the garage, makes travel impossible. Before retirement, he worked as a systems analyst for the Oregon Fish and Wildlife. Now he is a regular member of the Scotts Valley Senior Center, where he met my grandparents. My grandmother invited Steve, up to now a stranger to me, to take her ticket for a whale-watching cruise in Monterey Bay, which she decided she would skip a day or two before my visit, due to a bout of irritable bowel syndrome. My grandfather, well into his eighties, his mind now in the oncoming twilight of a gradual decline, sleeps while I ask polite questions of Steve, who drives us in his Prius through industrial-scale strawberry fields toward Moss Landing.

At Moss Landing, the twin, smokeless stacks of a natural gas power plant breast the bay. At dock, our whale-boat, and a research vessel named the *Rachel Carson*.

It is my first real time at sea. Once outside the mouth of the bay, land falls away and fog draws in. The floor of the ocean flips up like a shook tablecloth. What is most disorienting is its motional consistency. Which is to say its restlessness. No place for the eye to rivet but the horizon, an arbitrary line in the distance, abstract in its relativity to me.

I know I need to focus on that far-off line, or risk throwing up.

When we return home, whales witnessed, we find my grandmother sitting at the table with three thick, spiral-bound tomes, printed at Kinkos, and a bundle of file folders filled with material for a fourth. Her chronicles. The history of the Randall women. That of the Schumert line. Her autobiography. She leaves them for me to read.

I pretend to do so on the porch. But really, behind the covers of her book, I'm reading Hegel's *Phenomenology*. I am trying to learn that what emerges, emerges from itself, self-mediating on the way toward self-consciousness.

But it is a difficult, ongoing process. A dim series of dictions and contradictions. Arrivals met by departures. Time is its expression, until that time that nothing is outside. Utter internal coherence, or identity, which is to say singularity, which is to say simplicity. The simplicity of saying nothing at all. Saying's needlessness.

In the meantime, its needful complications. The needed frame, not to say nothing, but nothing's inverse. To say this is enough, to call it good, these red-gold reflections, an abstraction captured in a broken fish-trap.

The morning of my departure, we sit in the living room, the air smoky with blueberry pancakes burned by my grandfather, and she tells me memories she has of her mother, grandmother, and great grandmother fishing from the pier at Redondo Beach. She remembers also her childhood house on Juniper Lane, and asks if I would like to hear her read out loud the corresponding passage in her book. As preface, she says she wishes she was an artist, to be able to draw the house and its yard, so clearly they stand in her mind. She adds: "Instead, all I have is words":

> "Out of doors was a varied place. Cement right outside the laundry-door area, with a large cactus garden to the left—huge cacti in

all varieties. Some only bloomed at night. Outside the fenced area to the left was where the clothesline was, and where Grandmother's sweet peas grew. There was a large growth of pear cactus in the front yard as thick as a garden wall. Back inside the main yard if you went directly to the house you would be in the summerhouse. It is a framed area done in a type of lattice-work, sides and roof. In this summerhouse hung the most beautiful fuchsias and begonias you've ever seen. All these wonderful colors and birds, as well as the butterflies. On the ground was a carpet of tear-drop moss, where we didn't walk. Where we walked was a flat, stone walkway. There were ground-fuchsias also, and a picnic table was in the middle for eating, playing cards, and visiting. Outside this area to the left, looking to the house, was a bird aviary with small finches. Nana also had a few chickens for eggs. Down the steps to the lower part to the right was Billy's workshop. If you went the other way, on the left, to the path on the hillside, was peach-trees and flowers, but the best thing was the dirt cellar under the house. The dirt cellar was under most of the house, so it was quite large, and the smell was delicious. A mixture of dirt and I don't know what else, but I loved it. In the cellar, on the shelves, was Nana's canning. There were jars of spiced figs, spiced apples, pickles, peaches, albacore, berries, beans, et cetera. This is a place I was at almost daily as a child. I even had a little friend who lived in the only other house on that land. Her name was Shirley Fair. There were many huge California pepper-trees in this area that grew right down to the ground like weeping willows. We would take a water or a milk carton, and find a trap-door spider, open the door with a knife, and then pour the water in and out would come the spider."

When she gets to the fuchsias, my grandmother begins to weep.
Tear-drop moss where we couldn't walk.
A mixture of dirt and I don't know what else, but I loved it.
At first, I felt a kind of horror. How a simple house, minutely described, could come to spire in the mind like a temple. Holy the colors and birds, as well as the butterflies.
How simple the life.

Or: horrified that I knew this to be my life, too. Its similar details, impoverished because specific.

The taste of myself. My own spit on my skin.

Reproached for masturbating in public, Diogenes retorted, "If only one could put an end to hunger by rubbing one's stomach!"

I think what he meant is that you should take what you can get. Or that you should settle for what you can give yourself. His autoeroticism a performance of the limits of self-sufficiency.

One night, feeling sullen and sorry for himself because his arduous, unnatural lifestyle kept him from joining in the revelries of an Athenian festival, Diogenes was eating barley-cakes alone, when he noticed a mouse approaching to gather up his crumbs. A biographer of Greek philosophers recounts that the Cynic saw the mouse "running this way and that, not looking for anywhere to lie down, not having any fear of the dark, not yearning for any of the things that are regarded as desirable, and from its example, [Diogenes] discovered the way out of his difficulties."

Maybe what the philosopher learned from the mouse is that he was trying too hard. That the simple life was simply appetite and light, and from time to time light's absence, night. And that you can subsist on a crumb. And that daybreak is night's surface broken by a churn of golden bodies, hungry for crumbs cast from the hands of complex gods. Now it is morning, morning's nowness hollow as a storage jar in which there sleeps a single satisfying seed.

Gnats

After heavy rains eroded the ditch bank close to Bingham Hill cemetery and turned up the rotting casket of John Thomas, died 1877, the Rainbow Riders 4-H club took it upon themselves to do a service for the dead and move the grave. Storm-softened clay gave way easily. So did the coffin's sponge-wood. In life, John Thomas had bright red hair that still clung in tufts to the fragments of his skull, which lay on a sheaf of green pamphlets advertising tea. The deteriorating grave proved too difficult to move, so the 4-H club-members elected to reinter the body, wool socks still clinging to its foot-bones. They included in the coffin a note of apology. In 1989, an aspiring Eagle Scout rebuilt the ditch bank with railroad ties, and sealed John Thomas back into the hillside.

On visiting Rose at her ranch in LaPorte, Colorado, she offers to show me a shoebox with some of Thomas's red hair in it. She tells me that in all her time researching and caring for and living next to the small pioneer cemetery, which came with the land her husband bought to keep cattle in the seventies, Thomas's body was the only one whose bones she had held, whose hair she had touched.

Rose grew up in Nebraska and intends to be buried there when she dies. But she has spent much of her adult life in Colorado tracking down and identifying the bodies of strangers buried on her property. She has written and self-published a handbook history of the cemetery, which occupies 1.2 acres. You can see it at a distance from her kitchen window.

When I ask about her motivation in carrying on such morbid volunteer labor, she insists she's not a "cemetery nut." She doesn't "drive around the country looking for cemeteries." Instead, "it just happened that the timing was right," she tells me. "The placing was right. It was right here."

Until this morning, Rose was a stranger with whom I'd only exchanged a few emails to coordinate a meeting so we could talk about the cemetery and her book. Now, at her dining room table, while her adult son surfs the internet in the living room beside a hot wood-stove, she shows me a photo of her priest standing on a glacier in Iceland. She also shows me a photo of a pipeline being dug on her property and complains about the frackers in

Greeley buying river-water to mix with proppants and shoot at high speeds deep into drill-holes.

In truth, I made up a reason to be here. I told Rose, a woman nearing eighty, that I wanted to interview her for thesis research. I guess this is partly true, in the sense that "research" for a degree in poetry is an all-encompassing thing, and you can count drinking with friends in a bar until closing on a Tuesday night as readily as you can reading for broken sonnets in *Paradise Lost*.

I realize half-way through the conversation that the question I have come to ask has to do with allochthony, the opposite of autochthony, the latter meaning born from the earth, describing when a person springs up local from the dirt. Used as a demographic term, the word "allochthon," on the contrary, refers to one who "emerges from another soil." In geologic contexts, an allochthon is a landform displaced from its original position by a low angle thrust fault. Some of the foothills behind Rose's property, pitched toward the sky at a shorn angle, have been shoved up and broken off by similar drifting pressures. I think my question for this keeper of the pioneer dead is less about what it means to dwell in, and more what it means to care for a place where you didn't choose to be, or where you could never have foreseen being.

From Rose I want to know: how do you take as yours what has been given? Maybe your husband is a beef cattle geneticist at the agricultural college, and the parcel of rangeland he purchases to study livestock has perched upon on it, not far from the house where you raise your seven kids, a little plot of illegible headstones.

A drill-rig in the pasture. The intaglio of ditches in the valley. The person you sleep beside in bed. A life is a kind of dirt. You are supposed to feel autochthonous to it, as if you belonged to it. You don't have to think to take it for granted.

A year or so after meeting Rose, when I move from Colorado to North Carolina to study nineteenth-century American poetry, I start looking for gaps in the woodwork, fault-lines for fitting in. Parts of the intarsia I can loosen, slip between. But maybe a fit is not exactly what I'm after. What I'm looking for is a pattern, an infrastructure. Groundwork for a network for thought at speeds. In a new state, a new field for study, I want to move effortlessly, connectedly, as if to move was to more belong.

Passing clear-cut corridors for vaulting power-lines. Or on interstates and highways: pivoting through dense green walls of mixed deciduous and pine. I try to triangulate myself in a flattened landscape of strip mall, chapel, auto shop, tracking with the mills at intervals along the rivers that run tribute to Cape Fear. The Deep. The Haw. Mermaid Point, where they meet. To secure the network, I take walks through the North Forest near the university, listening to old oral history interviews with now-dead mill-workers that stream from the air into my iPhone. The dead tell me how if you worked in a spinning room you soon learned to read lips above the racket.

On the website *Find a Grave*, I learn some of the bodies of the voices in my ears are buried at a drivable distance. On a winter Saturday, I visit Burlington Memorial Gardens, seeking the graves of Henry A, Betty D. I listen to their interviews as I search. The grounds are larger than I thought they would be, and the office is closed, so I wander directionless and unrewarded between the headstones, gathering as a form of consolation sun-paled, mower-shredded fragments of false flowers, which I save in my coat pocket, as if I had some future purpose for them.

Over the next two years, I find my efforts as a scholar of nineteenth-century poetry are met with similar results. A pocketful of plastic pansies gathered from the grounds of a burial garden whose dirt conceals the bodies of strangers. The feeling of trying too hard to belong. Not sure what I'm searching for, I start to drift in my studies toward the twentieth century, as close to Pound and Eliot as I can come without crossing over into modernism, settling on a narrow range of years at the nineteenth century's end during which time books of poetry bore titles like "Thoughts," "Dewdrops," "Scribbles," "Trifles," "Daisies," "Violets," "Driftwood."

One critic describes the American poets of the 1890s archly as the "Household Furniture School." Theirs, the critic jokes, is the "poetry inherent in kitchen floors, kettles, clocks, rocking chairs, baby chairs, chimneys, cribs (trundle beds), cots, spinning wheels, and bureau drawers... [S]uch minutiae as old straw hats, shotguns, cigars, canteens, pipes, shoes, umbrellas, cucumber vines, beans, and even 'my last tooth.'" Surrounded by the ephemeral, substanceless, and commonplace, I find myself less in a field of viable study as much as in the midst of a yard sale or a rural midden, the contents of a household turned out on a weedy lawn, left to gather dewdrops overnight.

But whether it was written in 1890 or 1809, it's hard to know how to read a nineteenth-century American poem, Dickinson and Whitman the exception. Many of the century's most popular poems feel kindred to crochet, or lacy open-work. Their patterns are floral and ornate, but conventional. They are craft objects, pious and sparkly, circulating in the margins of newspapers, sentimental column filler for prose-focused periodicals. Ornaments for the off-hours. Small balm. "Wildflowers gathered for a Sick Friend." "The Sinless Child." "Death of an Infant."

For her own PhD dissertation, the scholar I study with wrote about three obscure nineteenth-century poetesses and their relationship to Edgar Allan Poe: Frances Sargent Osgood, Sarah Helen Whitman, and Elizabeth Oakes Smith. She later published the project as a well-regarded book. Despite this success, the scholar once confessed to me there was a time she wondered if so many years of intellectual labor on Osgood, Whitman, and Smith—writers essentially unknown to contemporary audiences—would be equivalent to aiming a cannon at a gnat.

Even as he was dying of consumption, Thoreau still stopped to study the growth patterns of ruderal weeds along the sand-banks of the railway that passed through his woods, inspecting little-noticed plants that flourish where the earth has been disturbed, displaced, laid waste, opened to infrastructure. I try to channel his ethic as I wander the forgotten lots, margins, medians, and waste-lands of the nineteenth-century poem. Digging in that dirt in an attempt to lay a route. Some way to be in them, by moving through them. Weeds spring up as a result.

> "But from the rock, rough-grained, and icy-crowned,
> Some little flower from out some cleft will rise;
> And in this quiet land my love I found,
> With all their soft light, sleepy, in her eyes.
>
> No bush to lure a bird to sing to her—
> In depths of calm the gnats' faint hum was drowned,
> And the wind's voice was like a little stir
> Of the uneasy silence, not like sound."

In November 1844, Edgar Allan Poe published a selection of jotted notes penciled in the margins of books pulled at random from the shelves of his personal library.

In the margins beside a sentence in a treatise on conic sections by Apollonius of Perga ("The right angle of light's incidence produces a sound upon one of the Egyptian pyramids"), Poe wrote:

"It is nonsense, I suppose, — but it will not do to speak hastily. The orange ray of the spectrum and the buzz of the gnat (which never rises above the second A), affect me with nearly similar sensations. In hearing the gnat, I perceive the color. In perceiving the color, I seem to hear the gnat."

To study gnats and hear a pyramid, slanted orange in the declining sun.

In the scrutinized buzz, a far-flung association. A cryptic monolith where before there was only an irritation at the ear.

Digging near the pyramid of Amenemhat III at Hawara, the British archeologist Flinders Petrie uncovered the mortuary labyrinth that Herodotus described: twelve covered courts, each containing three thousand rooms, half above ground, half below. Those below include "the tombs of the kings who built the labyrinth, and also the tombs of the sacred crocodiles"; the upper rooms of carved marble are, according to the ancient historian, "an endless wonder," full of "baffling and intricate passages from room to room and from court to court."

In the vicinity, Petrie also exhumed burial pits filled with the mummies of professional upper-class Greek-Egyptians. Many of the bodies were accompanied by vivid portraits painted in beeswax on panels of linden wood, depicting the faces of the dead, who, while still living, commissioned these likenesses to distinguish them in death. Petrie found that he could revitalize the colors—gold, black, red, two different ochres—by carefully heating the wax. Exposed to candle-warmth, faces flushed back to life, returning to that day they sat to have their portrait taken, gazing at the painter as one might gaze at death, hands clasped in their laps, feeling their own cool body heat.

Petrie is known for formalizing the archeological technique of seriation:

dating the layers of a dig-site based on fragments of upturned pottery. He remarked, "I believe the true line of research lies in the noting and comparison of the smallest details." As an eight-year-old, he overheard some family friends describing the recent frenzied excavation of the Brading Roman Villa, some of its mosaics found while a farmer was laying the foundations for his sheep-pens on the Isle of Wight. Preternaturally appalled by the careless treatment of the site, the boy "protested that the earth should be pared away, inch by inch, to see all that was in it and how it lay."

Along with the Labyrinth and the Fayum Portraits, Petrie also found at Hawara the unmarked, unadorned mummy of a young woman, her skull lying, like John Thomas's on the pile of rotting ads for tea, against a crumbled scroll that contained within it a copy of the second book of Homer's *Iliad*—the great gathering of armies, the catalogue of ships.

Near the beginning of Book Two, before the catalogue, Agamemnon tarries in a rare moment of self-reflective clarity, aware of his immoderate ambitions, and of his own defenselessness to willful gods:

"...but the son of Kronos
Zeus who bears the aegis, has rather brought me sorrows,
tossing me into insoluble quarrels and disputes.
For I and Achilles fought each other over a girl,
exchanging violent words, and my anger it was began it.
But if ever we reach agreement, from then no longer
shall the Trojans' doom be postponed, not for a moment!"

Despite his better angels, the king's lack of temperance prevailed, poor in that virtue the ancient Greeks called *sophrosyne*. So Agamemnon marshaled his men and did what he could with the information he had, slaughtering a five-year-old ox in the name of Zeus, to whom the offering meant nothing. It was this same god after all who tricked the Argive king into hastening this great gathering of armies, sending them to their collective doom. Yet divine intervention only worked in tandem with a deeper flaw, an irritable, grasping impulse to possess, the vast resources of a foreign kingdom mustered in pursuit of a substanceless dream. Cannons aimed at gnats, their thin, hallucinated song.

The ancient Greek poet Simonides was born on the island of Keos, which afforded a level of isolation from the wars and political turmoil that gripped the mainland. Due to the island's disconnectedness, the "air" there was noted for what one nineteenth-century classicist described as its "moral purity" (absent as it was of "courtesan and flute-girl"), and so Simonides was known to some for his *sophrosyne*, his perfect poise. A well-balanced life, gifted from geography. Yet the trouble with moral purity is that it produces "excessive longevity and consequent overpopulation"—and so at a certain age the inhabitants of Keos, unlike those belonging to other Greek states, who "relieved their congestion by the colonial route," chose to follow "what we may call the hemlock route."

D, a former teacher of mine, now a close friend, has recently finished translating from ancient Greek six lyric poets, including Simonides. One fragment addresses the difficulty of maintaining, especially when making things, the virtue of balance or *sophrosyne*: "Difficult to build by hand a man / truly good and well-built and with a mind, / four-square and made without a flaw…" Building, as it turns out, has nothing to do with it: "Good luck lets any man be good, / But if luck is bad, the man is bad." Simonides was autochthonous, native to good earth, and so he, too, was good. His goodness leads him to the following conviction:

"And so I don't waste my strength
to seek in hollow things meaning, I don't
throw my life away on impossible hopes—
…I applaud and love any man
who knowingly shuts himself away
and does nothing shameful."

Together walking the converted, now-verdant rail spur of the High Line in New York, on the lookout for a bite to eat and a drink, I confess to D that I have found it is hard to love the best-loved poems of the nineteenth century. With their too-simple clarity, they often resist my desire to read them deeply, and find in them some thought that re-surfaces the world around me, its landscape newly shifted, split. Unlike poems that promise what Rimbaud famously called a "derangement of the senses," their lack of complication makes them somehow indistinct, ungraspable, non-adhesive—less-than-gossamer structures. I hold hungrily to the littlest kink or swerve in the language. To D I describe the process of looking for something to love in them as a kind of *askesis*, an exhausting practice. Sounding for lighter-than-air pyramids in the barest buzzing octave of a gnat.

And I confess that the decision to work in this field, in this nineteenth-century dirt, was never something to which I gave much thought. Instead, in the care of certain teachers, it just happened that the timing was right. The placing was right. It was right here. Over time, I found myself laboring in a foreign land, whose virtues were not mine, not having sprung from its earth.

Lizette Woodworth Reese, an all-but-forgotten poet and school-teacher from Baltimore, Maryland, where Edgar Allan Poe is buried, helped bridge the transition from the nineteenth-century's violets tied with string and pansies to modernism's harsh, hard-cut images, its "spice-rose / drip[ping] such acrid fragrance / hardened in a leaf," as H.D. puts it in one poem. One scholar has celebrated both Reese's "exquisite simplicity" and her *sophrosyne*, describing her "ability, despite the genius which set her apart, to fit in with all phases of life. She made adjustments so well that more than once she was called 'unimpressing.'"

Less a life than a series of adaptions and adjustments. Which is a life. A well-balancing.

She saw a garden as a place of law, of "fixity," and the "sureness of things":

"A snowdrop is always white, and forever holds that green tip on the edge; a jonquil always cupped in gold. This is the law of the place. You are struck a hard blow; perhaps it is the breaking into pieces of an old dream, or the death of a friend, or the treachery of one whom you trusted as you trusted yourself. At first the world staggers under you, [as] you try to settle yourself into the hard and bitter new order of things. And yet everything in the garden goes on as before. Even the dry sound of a seedpod cracking open—as tiny a business as that —remains. This changelessness at first is one of the most bewildering of human experience…But—after a while it is this very changelessness which works your cure. To look out and see that unquenched blaze of scarlet geraniums in a corner of your garden is to see a candle to light you on your way. A sense of the continuity of life, the keeping on of affairs, of the certain security of the incomings and outwanderings of nature comes to you. Here is a staff to lean upon, a crook to clutch. Here are the everlasting arms."

The snowdrop, daisy, and violet: timeless in their vibrancy, changeless in their plasticity. Perhaps the law of the garden holds as true for a handful of plastic flowers culled from the cut lawn of strange graves. Or for the tiny business of dewdrops and driftwood. Of lacework and gnats. Perhaps these, too, can help you settle yourself. To come to rest in the midst of green tips and permanent gold cups thrusting up from a restless earth.

In 1891, as Flinders Petrie was excavating the Great Temple of Aten on the banks of the Nile, Reese published a poem called "Love, Weeping, Laid this Song" in her book *A Handful of Lavender*. The poem bears a subtitle: "On a copy of the *Iliad* found with the mummy of a young girl." The rest reads as follows, here in its entirety:

"Lo! an old song, yellow with centuries!
She, she who with her young dust kept it sweet;
She, in some green court on a carved seat,
Read it at dusk fair-paged upon her knees;
And, looking up, saw there, beyond the trees
Tall Helen through the darkling shadows fleet;
And heard, out in the fading river-street,
The roar of battle like the roar of seas.
Love, weeping, laid this song when she was dead
In that sealed chamber, strange with nard and musk.
Outliving Egypt, see it here at last.
We touch its leaves: back rush the seasons sped;
For us, as once for her, in that old dusk,
Troy trembles like a reed before the blast!"

It is Reese's reconstruction of the dead girl's distant imagination that revitalizes the *Iliad*'s yellow song. We re-read Agamemnon's false dream by the dim light of the girl's eyes, brightened back into living color by the candle-warmth of Reese's poem. For us, as once for her: what Homer saw.

From out of the substanceless terrain of a late century, I lend a hand at excavating Reese, who helps excavate a little reader, who in turn unburies for us Helen from the shade-trees. Mind spading into mind spading into mind. A daisy-chain of digging, but not, it must be said, in dirt. To read, not by light, nor any vision of my own, but a vision seen through the trees, a luminous dusk-dream. The pages brightened by being buried underneath the head of a nameless girl, Greek, allochthonous, entombed in Egypt—and then exhumed, decrypted.

For his part, blind Homer died undone, benighted, unable to solve a too-simple riddle posed to him by some fisher-boys by the sea-shore: "We left whatever we caught and carry whatever we didn't." It wasn't fish they meant.

Nor a pocketful of false flowers, deathless plastic-polyester petals.

Trying to hear pyramids where there are only gnats.

For the answer to the riddle after all was lice. Something small as that.

Not knowing it was a simple louse he combed his brain for, as one might red hair, Homer perished of despair.

A Perfect Summer Life

Twice refracted by water and glass, sunlight passes through a vase and falls onto the table where it webs with color like an iris, or your vision when you break the surface of a lake, blind and blinking through a wetted mesh. On the other wall, a darker transfer, shadow of mixed seasonals, bobbing pom and tulip leaf. Sensing shallowness, terror in the opposite of drowning, I look for reassurance in the light and its effects: what gives depth, dimension, surfaces that shade away, some of every object self-concealed behind its glinting rim, what was half-emptied now half-full, knowing that there's more to it. To this, this careless collection, ewer and flintlock, cameo and gourd. In a still life, it is the light that tells us how to feel about the tipped pitchers, lolling hares, and clotted nectarines, infusing with tone and mood what is otherwise dead, jumbling the frame in random aggregate. Chasing everything with gold, light tells the angle that the sun is at, low to the horizon, and how little time there is to view this scene, image in which nothing in particular is happening. A white cabbage butterfly has come to rest forever on a grape, forever depositing its gnawing egg. The linoleum covering the kitchen floor is water-warped and peeling up. Boxes from our recent move remain unpacked. It is the first time I have shared a house with the same person with whom I also share a bed, too hot for sheets. We haven't gotten around yet to buying curtains for the big sliding glass doors in our bedroom, so in the mornings, I wake with the light, lying on my side, facing the hollow roar from a nearby road.

At the end of *Walden*, as he moves out of his cabin by the pond, Henry David Thoreau promises that "there is an incessant influx of novelty into the world." He says so impatient with people who aren't where they are, who can't seem to love what they have, life that in fact teems and seethes, weevil in the wheat. As proof, he tells the story of a Massachusetts farmer and his family, who, sitting one night around their dinner table, were astonished to find a "strong and beautiful bug" had hatched and chewed itself free of the apple-tree wood out of which the table had been fashioned over sixty years before. Apparently, heat from a pot set down had been enough to finally awaken the worm, still living, quickened in its carapace. "Who knows what beautiful and winged life," Thoreau concludes, "whose egg has been buried for ages under many concentric layers of woodenness in the dead dry life of society, deposited at first in the alburnum of the green and living tree, which has been gradually converted into the semblance of its well-seasoned tomb,—heard perchance gnawing out now for years by the astonished family of man, as they sat round the festive board,—may unexpectedly come forth from amidst society's most trivial and handselled furniture, to enjoy its perfect summer life at last!" That life, moth-light, and only as long as the day that it was hatched, decrypted by the warmth of a shared meal at table or tomb.

Thoreau ends his experiment in living a life of "simplicity, simplicity, simplicity" by leaving the woods. Or perhaps it would be more accurate to say that, coming out of the woodwork, he enters his life at last, his gnawing finally over, obsessive study of a little pond or "iris," so described for possessing two colors, "one when viewed at a distance, and another, more proper, close at hand." It isn't clear why this property of water brings to Thoreau's mind the eye's anatomy, except perhaps that it is the eye or its level that determines the spectrum of light it will receive, refracted then reflected off the pond. Leaving our new home to visit Concord just days after we move, I wade to my neck into Walden while K dives in. I try to lay my eye on a plane with its, hoping to observe the binary blue and green that Thoreau insists is the special index of this water. I strain to get a glimpse of the illusion, of "the matchless and indescribable light blue, such as watered or changeable silks and sword blades suggest, more cerulean than the sky itself, alternating with the original dark green on the opposite sides of the waves, which last appeared but muddy in comparison." Thinking that my angle might be wrong, too close to catch the effect, I wade back, stand up, peer down: the water is clear enough to watch tiny fish approach my legs, distorted by transparency, to kiss or taste them. In the distance, laughter, thin and buzzing music from a bluetooth. Closer by, the smell of pot and something rotting in the reeds. Though K tries to coax me in, I don't immerse myself. I stay on the surface, trying to see an eye, its complex cusp, where there is only clarity.

"For the most part," writes Thoreau, "we are not where we are, but in a false position." One word for this is ecstasy: to stand outside the self, its tedious circumference. Or maybe what Thoreau condemns us for is ecstasy in negative: we live, for the most part, outside the self, and it is truer transport to return, radius reduced, the eye adjusting to the sudden flood of light by narrowing. We are where we are, morning in a shared bed, sharing supper at the table, though thought would tell us otherwise, that "infinity of our natures" or incessant reckoning process by which "we suppose a case, and put ourselves into it, and hence are in two cases at the same time, and it is doubly difficult to get out." Thought, then, amounting to refusal, sum of this world plus some other, world in which I wake inside a double-wide in Wamsutter, deep inside the heartland or the thick of things, thick unhollow heartwood, hidden there among the joinery and furniture.

Hidden anywhere but here. I look outside the window where I read and read, peering into the green seethe, the wooded gulley between us and what I know to be the road, though I can't see it through the leaves. In Hume I read: "Philosophy would render us entirely Pyrrhonian," by which I think he means that if we let it, we would think ourselves into a slough or ditch, stumbling on pyrrhic feet, as in the first and third foot in this Googled line, both syllables unstressed: "To a | green thought | in a | green shade."

Here, the pyrrhic work of prepositions, indefinite determiners. Words with which to orient, gain footing, enter and dwell. To love the person you find each night you sleep beside. And by you here I mean me. I mean I am here by you. That is, thanks to, and beside you. Eye to eye, but at an angle, your eye appears depending on the angle that I'm at, over here, in this false position, not where I should be, which is to say, not as close at hand as I pretend.

And yet, it is the first summer that I don't put distance between us, visit friends in other states, traverse continents to see things in a different light, across a gap. Instead, I sit in a new and unfamiliar room, K somewhere downstairs, and read that what saves us from our tendency to doubt the reality or certainty of our perceptions is the "assent-salvaging" feature of the imagination. To be able to say yes, not because it makes sense to, but for the simple fact that the mind literally cannot help believing that what's there is there.

That that's that.

But, of course, it isn't. I mean, it isn't over, never is. Philosophy, by which Hume means "refined and metaphysical reasoning," would render us Pyrrhonian, save the fact that the mind can't help but see causation, make associations, draw connections, saying yes to the world in such a way as to render it seamlessly consistent, one thing always leading to the next. The problem with reason and reflection—that is to say, with thought—is that it suspends this otherwise natural or automatic process, makes what is smooth seem discontinuous, tries to ascertain the gap between Point A and Point B and understand what drove trajectory. In this way, the mind insures itself against illusion and tricks of the eye, but at the price of analysis, exhaustive interrogation. According to Hume, to know which of my imaginings are real and which are false, I have to keep on correcting, correcting my corrections, because in reality I have no access to a world outside the world I see, and so there is no perfect surety. There are only approximations, approaches, and the process of securing these involves an infinite regression from whatever place I started from, whatever first intensity. In autumn, in the vineyard with its ordered rows beside the house where I grew up, "the grapes made sharp air sharper by their smell." It is a sensual intensity that suffers as soon as I start to think about it, mapping onto the original experience a line from a poem by Wallace Stevens, in which the poet speculates on the aftermath of a volcanic eruption. Though I read the poem long after leaving home and its vineyard, it has since rerouted whatever memories I still retain of Concord grapes, affording them a sinus sharpness, image of clarity, forehead cleared of fog. Now traced, this distillation of intensity, of mists dispersed, begins to dissipate, re-attenuate, absorbed into the line by Stevens like sunlight through a bank of fog, diffusing across a mass of particles or points, the point or points of this, this fuzziness of origin.

If you start from Thoreau's birth-site, a farm his family lost due to crop failure during one of two consecutive "years without a summer," summer that Thoreau was born, and head toward Concord's town center, you will pass a tombstone-shaped monument outside a white colonial cottage, marking not a death, but the origins of a grape-variant bred to withstand subzero New England winter temperatures. Embellished with a frieze in half-relief of grapes, grapevines, and trellis posts, the stone reads: "Ephraim Wales Bull planted seeds of a wild Labrusca grape found growing on this hillside which, after three generations, through his work and wisdom, became in this garden in September 1840 the Concord Grape." A cutting of the original vine still grows near the edge of the cottage property. The Concord grape is good for making jellies and sacramental wine. Sometimes it is used as a table-grape. I search the internet for paintings of the fruit, small and dark and potent. Almost, it seems to me, ubiquitous in still life, homage to those by Zeuxis, so like the life that they drew birds from the sky to peck at them, the grapes I'm used to seeing on tables and in the midst of silver bowls and broken plinths are larger, almost Canaanite, and frequently so ripe they glow from the inside out, more lucent and less recent than this American variant. But soon enough I dig up a painting by an Indiana portraitist named Barton Hays, dated at the turn of the twentieth century, featuring such clusters on a small porcelain plate, bunched up cloth beneath it. Some of these Concord grapes, normally pale with a whitish film of yeast, have been rubbed to a richer, darker shine, evidence of handling, plucked and then arranged, the painter choosing, or, in staying true to life, not choosing, to retain the trace of his touch.

Anciently, pictures like this one, of fruits or vegetables or meat and tinctured drink, hung in the foyers and hallways of estates in ancient Greece, creating a series of inviting images that were supposed to anticipate the plenty that awaited guests and strangers on the inside. An enticement to enter deeper in. As if to say, at the end of this, I promise, there is something good to eat, a laden table, somewhere to sit and rest from wandering from A and B.

It is at such a table that Hume took comfort after working himself up into a nervous wreck, his mind undone with doubts connected with his philosophizing. Having proven the radical disconnect between mind and world, Hume wonders anxiously: "Where am I, or what? From what causes do I derive my existence, and to what condition shall I return? Whose favour shall I court, and whose anger must I dread? What beings surround me? and on whom have I any influence, or who have any influence on me? I am confounded with all these questions, and begin to fancy myself in the most deplorable condition imaginable, inviron'd with the deepest darkness, and utterly depriv'd of the use of every member and faculty."

Thankfully, though: "Nature cures me of this melancholy or delirium either by relaxing this bent of mind, or by some avocation, and lively impression of my senses, which obliterate all these chimeras." Eventually, that is, "I dine, I play a game of back-gammon, I converse, and am merry with my friends; and [afterwards] these speculations ... appear so cold, and strain'd, and ridiculous, that I cannot find it in my heart to enter into them any farther."

Merry with his friends, sharing table-grapes and wine, Hume realizes he has gnawed himself, not into clarity, but a kind of relief, half-emerging from the background, tombstone carved with trellises and vines. The relief of staying for a while on the surface, not trying to pry too deeply into things, simplicity the grave and graven consequence of overthinking it, "it" with reference to simplicity itself.

When I show him an essay I have written called "A Simple Life," my friend D writes back, "Somehow I feel in your essay a working out of what honesty is, and some sense that the simple abides there, in that honesty. What is most curious in your essay is how often it is secretly an essay about companionship. The presence of the other that trues you to the fact of the world as it is contingent to or outside the scope of your mind. I think I mean to say only that the presence of the other keeps the world in a mutual place, belonging to neither, mutually shared, an ongoing work of agreeing on the facts as they unconceal themselves. The labyrinth of the mind and the fact of the world and how they tangle and untangle one another."

The unconcealing of a moth or cabbage butterfly as a consequence of dinnertime. Consequence the very notion Hume is famous for dismantling. And then, exhausted, sought thoughtlessness in company.

Afraid, I think, of her closeness, unable, so close, to see eye to eye, her eye dissolving into a simple clarity with kissing fish, I left K the summer before moving in with her to visit friends in Utah.

Leaving Provo in the late afternoon, Z and I had tried to time it so that we would reach the Spiral Jetty around sundown, at which hour and angle the light would have leveled both the Salt Lake's surface and its distant rim of mountains pink, undoing any difference between that horizon and the immediate radius of a swimmer's reach. Neither distance nor proximity. Here as good as there. Salt-suspension at the center of an orb the color of a fist hiding the beam of a flashlight. But the jetty was further than we thought, and at the end of a long road ribbed with axle-bashing potholes. So, by the time we arrived, the light was nearly gone, and the water and the sky had taken on a wine-dark consistency.

Still, we waded in, floated on our backs, buoyant and breathing easily in the high saline until true nightfall.

We had remembered to bring gallons of tap-water to bathe with after swimming, because otherwise the salt would rime our lips and ears. On the banks of a dead lake, we washed each other in the dark, a kind of second baptism, neither of us Mormon anymore. Except for the manmade jetty, the shoreline's seeping tar and barrenness, which tapers into high desert and subsequent rangeland, prohibits much in the way of human construction. So it is lightless below, numberless above.

Turning back, we passed for a second time the Golden Spike, site of the joined rails of the First Transcontinental Railroad in the spring of 1869, and from there dipped toward the outlying shimmer of Salt Lake City's valley lights. Retrograding into cell service, my phone lit up with several worried messages. K, a continent away, not knowing why she couldn't reach me, had feared—unreasonably, I felt—the worst. Soon after I had hung up, Z received a calmer call from his wife at home, who informed him that she was going to bed, and that their two children were also sleeping. On the interstate, he told me that they loved each other for their separate lives. For example, he had taken to driving long hours for Lyft and had even rented a tiny studio at an artist's community in town where he wrote poetry and sometimes slept.

Later, in the fall and home again, I got a call from Z, who told me that he takes it back, it isn't true. You can't lead separate lives. There is always an attenuation, an angling away, imperceptible until it isn't, and then the distance can at last be calculated, as if by parallax. He told me his wife has fallen in love with someone else, and that they would soon be divorced. After moving out of the small house that he once shared with his family, Z lived for a while out of his car, and on his friends' couches. He got a tattoo—two inked letters, "W.W.," for Walt Whitman—on his right hand east of his thumb-joint, in the little saddle where a pen might rest while the writer waits for something to say. Often he took pictures of this hand holding colorful blossoms found on long walks going nowhere, the tattoo visible, and posted these to social media. A year after his divorce, he flew to Portland, Maine, and set out on a 100-mile walk to Boston. Overambitious, assuming his own exhaustlessness, he went too far his first day, gave himself a stress fracture in his left foot, and had to take a train the rest of the way south.

Trying to get too quickly from point A to point B, or anywhere.

Hume says the human mind runs on associations, and for this reason risks seduction by appearances and images, false consistencies. In fact, anything can relate to anything. The French philosopher Henri Bergson: "For we should seek in vain for two ideas which have not some point of resemblance, or which do not touch each other somewhere."

Passing the cottage of Ephraim Wales Bull, goldbeater turned viticulturalist, I pick a grape from the original Concord mother-vine, wrap it in a napkin so it doesn't prematurely burst, and stow it in my book-bag. Watching me, K draws an association between two fruits and two pilgrimages, and asks if I still have the plum I picked two years ago from the tree in front of John Keats's house in Hampstead Heath, which is where I like to think he wrote his "Ode to a Nightingale."

As we walk, she asks me to connect the grape and the plum. Easy, I say; what they have in common is volcanoes.

If it's true what Bergson says, that "however profound are the differences which separate two images, we shall always find, if we go back high enough, a common genus to which they belong," then what is it that holds any two thoughts together? What determines the direction of series of associations, or the bundling of perceptions that Hume calls the self?

Hume's response: the passions. Our passions, stemming from pain and pleasure, flowering into love and hate, pride and shame, fructifying into projects, goals and intentions. These give direction to our thoughts, make the sharp air sharper.

The smell of the grape: a briar in space, a mist of every particle and particular coming to a point.

To wander in this mist, pyrrhic-footed. The horizon vanishes. Here as good as there.

Grounded again only by a little wine with friends. A round of backgammon. Any game but this one.

What's more, the passions, Hume argues, are social: "the minds of men are mirrors to one another, not only because they reflect each other's emotions, but also because those rays of passions, sentiments and opinions may be often reverberated."

You can't lead separate lives.

When Mt. Tambora erupted in 1815, on the island of Sumbawa in the Dutch East Indies, the veil of volcanic ash it sent up set in motion a short climate depression with devastating global effects, which lasted until 1819.

Thoreau was born in Concord on July of 1817, in the middle of a cold summer of crop failures. He lived for eight months in his birth-home down the street from Bull and Emerson, in whose foyer hangs a painting of Vesuvius, before the climate crisis set in motion by Tambora caused the farm to fold and forced his family to move. They didn't go far, just up the road, but it precipitated a lifetime of itinerancy within a tiny radius: in his forty years in Concord, Thoreau lived in over a dozen different homes.

In July of 1818, Keats contracted tuberculosis while nursing his brother Tom, who was dying of the same disease, and perhaps acquired it while the Keats brothers were living in poor, unwholesome urban conditions during 1816, year without a summer.

In colder, low-humidity contexts, aerosols from a cough or outburst (of laughter, anger) can remain suspended in the air for up to several minutes. A reduced photoperiod, compounded by vasoconstriction of the upper respiratory system, which could stem from chilled feet.

Wallace Stevens' poem, "Postcard from a Volcano," is a testimony of the post-apocalypse as spoken by the choric dead. All we know is that a catastrophic eruption has occurred. The poem begins in the ancient history of its aftermath: "Children picking up our bones / Will never know that these were once / As quick as foxes on the hill; // And that in autumn, when the grapes / Made sharp air sharper by their smell / These had a being, breathing frost."

Etymologically, "apocalypse" means "revelation." To speak of post-apocalypse is to speak of that period of time during which the sharp pangs of revelation dull into the day-to-day realities of life in the aftermath, in the shadow of ash. In time, children run around, here and there picking up a femur, a metatarsal, a skull with shattered sinuses. The world sinks back again into the easy routines of not-knowing that preceded the disaster. The iris adjusts. Transience itself becomes a habit, a set and silent bone. You forget just how it came to this, spitting toothpaste at dawn onto the asphalt of the parking lot where you had spent the night sleeping in your car.

What the grape and plum have in common is a let-down. I mean, their being held in common is itself a disappointment. The apocalypse, the appearance of a volcano on our way from Thoreau's birthplace to Walden Pond, renders the day no differently. We are still en route. Later we will wade into the water and try to give ourselves over to the illusion that "Walden is blue at one time and green at another, even from the same point of view," its iridescence answering to our stillness, our staying put while the surface seethes beneath us. "We walk on molten lava," Emerson wrote in his journal in 1832, "on which the claw of a fly or the fall of a hair makes its impression which being received, the mass hardens to flint & retains its impression forevermore." Beneath the resting cabbage butterfly will stabilize the grape. What is touchable and real, forming underneath the dust or yeast that settles on it. The ash in your hair, your hair in the shower, and trapped and burning wrapped around the rotor of the vacuum cleaner.

Outside the Keats House in Hampstead, children in school uniform, green and white, screamed and laughed, hollering memorized lines of dramatic verse to each other in groups of two or three. I wasn't able to tell who had written the lines as I strained to overhear them through a window from inside the house, near a glass case containing an oval brooch, a gem made of gold and resin to secure a tiny lyre strung with strands of Keats's hair. Designed by the painter Joseph Severn, who attended Keats in his dying moments in Rome, the jewel was intended for Fanny Brawne, the poet's fiancée, though Severn ultimately decided to keep it in the family, giving it to his own daughter as a marriage gift, remembering a new and not a broken union.

Beneath its bead of glass, the hair is ultrathin and white or blond with time. If plucked or even touched, the fine tied lines would surely snap, instrument unstrung by song. I found the object quaint and lurid all at once, or lurid in its quaintness, the poet reduced to a memento, a mere souvenir. Disturbed by the shallowness of the place, I wandered out of the house and approached the plum tree in the front yard. The children had vanished. It was early summer, and the fruit on the tree was still hard and green, but I picked one anyway, and hid it in my shoulder-bag. A nearby plaque informed me that this was not the same plum tree that the poet may have rested underneath while listening to nightingales; it was only an approximation, a fruitful shadow. I sat beside it anyway. Wetness seeped up from the grass and soaked the seat of my jeans.

In front of me, on my desk, lie three shriveled fruits: a grape from Concord, a plum from Hampstead, and a hickory nut that K brought back from Herman Melville's house at Arrowhead. In the grips of desiccation, they are barely distinguishable from one another, dark and mummified, forming in miniature a blackened still life where I write. I think I am most surprised that after all these years they have not attracted ants or other insects, or even mold. It seems that they have gnawed themselves.

Celebrating solitude, Thoreau observes how, even in the woods, his hut still swarms with visitors. Finding the little cabin empty, friends and neighbors will tend to leave a calling card or "wreath of evergreen, or a name in pencil on a yellow walnut leaf or a chip." Thoreau continues: "They who come rarely to the woods take some little piece of the forest into their hands to play with by the way, which they leave, either intentionally or accidentally. One has peeled a willow wand, woven it into a ring, and dropped it on my table." As if in disregard of his retreat, the surface of the humble wood or marble balustrade is strewn with twigs and droppings, even, perhaps, a berry or a walnut, here and there a grape. It is a small and unexpected meal, prepared by chance and distraction, the remains of what you take along with you to pass the time, and leave behind, careless in your care. These fragments of the outer world brought absent-minded in, and forming there a little network, nest of willow-branch and hair.

At the end of a day spent "botanizing" among the plants in solitude, cataloguing each specimen minutely in his journal, Thoreau exults: "My inheritance is not narrow." He adds, proud to have seen no one on his greedy rounds: "Here is no other this evening…There are said to be two thousand inhabitants in Concord, and yet I find such ample space and verge, even miles of walking every day in which I do not meet nor see a human being, and often not very recent traces of them." A micro-itinerancy, an entire life in Concord, wandering only as far as his legs could carry him. Restlessness within a tiny radius.

Weed to weed. Fever-bush to nightshade. An endless record of them. Wealth of live-forever, balsam fir, black spruce, and three-seeded mercury. Treasured up, this sugar maple, common yarrow, sweet flag, and horse chestnut, all in spitting distance of a clump of common winterberry, northern water plantain, hollyhock and amaranth. This prostrate pigweed, this prince's feather, ragweed, Roman wormwood, shadbush, hog peanut, pearly everlasting, big and little bluestem, mouse-ear, pussytoes, mayweed, common apple, one-flowered cancer root, groundnut, spreading dogbane, Drummond's rock cress, bearberry, side-flowering sandwort, jack-in-the-pulpit, China aster, late purple aster, calico aster, savory-leaved aster, small white aster, wavy-leaved aster, white wood aster:

A spreading ground of stars, numberless below. Point to point in constellation, reading in the angle of their barest shift from me or me from them how far I am from anything. I read and read. But not to put a distance between us. To find instead in constellating, in this bundling and clustering: a stumbling footing. In this narrow radius, a sprawling inheritance. A life in one place. Us, plus a few of our friends. The dinner-table laid, a warm pot set against its applewood, this and that thrown in, gumbo with whatever is on hand.

That gnawing you hear? For once it isn't coming from me.

Selected List of Works Consulted

Adnan, Etel. *Sea and Fog*. New York: Nightboat Books, 2012.

Beachy-Quick, Dan. *An Impenetrable Screen of Purest Sky: A Novel*. Minneapolis: Coffee House Press, 2013.

Beachy-Quick, Dan. *Stone-Garland*. Minneapolis: Milkweed Editions, 2020.

Beiser, Frederick C. *Diotima's Children: German Aesthetic Rationalism from Leibniz to Lessing*. Oxford: Oxford University Press, 2009.

Boruch, Marianne. *The Little Death of Self: Nine Essays Toward Poetry*. Ann Arbor: University of Michigan Press, 2017.

Brinks, Rose L. *History of the Bingham Hill Cemetery*. LaPorte: Self Published, 2015.

Bryson, Norman. *Looking at the Overlooked: Four Essays on Still Life Painting*. Cambridge: Harvard University Press, 1990.

Cary, Alice, and Phoebe Cary. *The Poetical Works of Alice and Phoebe Cary*. Boston: Houghton, Mifflin, 1882.

Clemens, Raymond, editor. *The Voynich Manuscript*. New Haven: Beinecke Rare Book & Manuscript Library, Yale University Press, 2016.

Constantine, David. *Holderlin*. Oxford: Clarendon, 1988.

Deleuze, Gilles. *Empiricism and Subjectivity: An Essay on Hume's Theory of Human Nature*. New York: Columbia University Press, 1991.

Deleuze, Gilles. *Dialogues II*. New York: Columbia University Press, 2007.

Diogenes, *Sayings and Anecdotes: With Other Popular Moralists*, edited by Robin Hard. Oxford: Oxford University Press, 2012.

Donahue, Thomas. *A Guide to Musical Temperament*. Lanham: Scarecrow Press, 2005.

Drower, Margaret S. *Flinders Petrie: A Life in Archaeology*. Madison: University of Wisconsin Press, 1995.

Essinger, James. *Jacquard's Web: How a Hand-Loom Led to the Birth of the Information Age*. Oxford: Oxford University Press, 2004.

Gadamer, Hans-Georg. "The History of Concepts and the Language of Philosophy." *International Studies in Philosophy* 18, no. 3 (1986): 1-16.

Gisbourne, Mark. "Baroque Decisions: the Inflected World of Adrian Ghenie" in *Adrian Ghenie*, ed. Juerg Judin, Ostfildern: Hatje Cantz, 2014.

Hadjithomas, Joana, and Khalil Joreige. "My Influences." *Frieze*, 1 May 2012.

Hegel, G.W.F. *Hegel's Phenomenology of Spirit*. Translated by A.V. Miller. Oxford: Oxford University Press, 1977.

Heraclitus, *On All Things*. Translated by Dan Beachy-Quick. (Unpublished).

Homer. *The Iliad: A New Translation by Peter Green*. Translated by Peter Green, Univ of California Press, 2015.

Jocelin of Furness. *Ancient Lives of Scottish Saints: Kentigern*. Translated by W.M. Metcalf, Llanerch Publishers, 1895 [1998].

Kindilien, Carlin T. *American Poetry in the Eighteen Nineties; a Study of American Verse, 1890-1899, Based upon the Volumes from That Period Contained in the Harris Collection of American Poetry and Plays in the Brown University Library*. Providence: Brown University Press, 1956.

Leibniz, Gottfried Wilhelm. "On an Instrument or Great Art of Thinking" in *Sämtliche schriften und briefe series VI, volume 4*. Translated by Lloyd Strickland. Darmstadt: O. Reichl, 1923.

Leibniz, Gottfried Wilhelm. *G.W. Leibniz's Monadology: An Edition for Students*. Edited and translated by Nicholas Rescher. Pittsburgh: University of Pittsburgh Press, 1991.

Manatt, J. Irving. *Aegean Days*. London: John Murray, 1913.

Mastai, Marie-Louise d'Otrange. *Illusion in Art : Trompe l'oeil, a History of Pictorial Illusionism*. New York: Abaris Books, 1975.

Miller, Eric. "Celadon's Russell Used Hard Work, Luck To Build Large Cross-Border TL Carrier." *Transport Topics*, 24 June 2014.

Morton, Timothy. *Hyperobjects: Philosophy and Ecology after the End of the World*. Minneapolis: University of Minnesota Press, 2013.

O'Leary, Peter. *Gnostic Contagion: Robert Duncan and the Poetry of Illness*. Wesleyan University Press, 2002.

Plutarch, and Edward N. O'Neil. *Moralia, vol. 5*. Translated by Frank Cole Babbitt, et al. Cambridge: Harvard University Press, 1927.

Quinn, D. Michael. *Early Mormonism and the Magic World View*. Salt Lake City: Signature Books, 1998.

Raggio, Olga, and Antoine M. Wilmering. *The Gubbio Studiolo and Its Conservation*. New York: Metropolitan Museum of Art, 1999.

Reese, Lizette Woodworth. *In Praise of Common Things: Lizette Woodworth Reese Revisited*, edited by Robert J. Jones. Westport, Connecticut: Greenwood Press, 1992.

Rescher, Nicholas. *Leibniz and Cryptography: An Account on the Occasion of the Initial Exhibition of the Reconstruction of Leibniz's Cipher Machine*. Pittsburgh: University Library System, 2013.

Revell, Donald. "Lecture by Donald Revell," *Poem Present*, The University of Chicago, 2009.

Richards, Eliza. *Gender and the Poetics of Reception in Poe's Circle*. Cambridge: Cambridge University Press, 2004.

Richardson, Robert D.. *Emerson: The Mind on Fire*. Berkeley: University of California Press, 2015.

Robertson, Lisa, "Etel Adnan," *Bomb Magazine* 127, April 2014.

Salto, Axel. *Den Spirende Stil*. Copenhagen: J.H. Schultz, 1959.

Smith, Elizabeth Oakes. *The Sinless Child, and Other Poems*. New York: Wiley & Putnam, 1843.

Sylvestre, Loïc, and Marco Costa. "The mathematical architecture of Bach's the Art of Fugue." *Il Saggiatore Musicale*, vol. 17, no. 2, 2010, pp. 175-195.

Thoreau, Henry David. *Thoreau's Wildflowers*. Edited by Geoff Wisner. New Haven: Yale University Press, 2016.

Acknowledgements:

Many thanks to *Tupelo Quarterly, Full Stop Quarterly, Black Sun Lit, rivulet, Ghost Proposal* and *Booth* for publishing some of these essays.

For their assistance in bringing *Incryptions* to print, special thanks to Dan Beachy-Quick, Maddison Colvin, Kristen Case, and the incredible editors at Spuyten Duyvil.

For generously reading early versions of the manuscript for this book, my gratitude to Carly Schnitzler, Jo Klevdal, and Meagan Wilson.

Thanks, also, to the friends without whom I could not have written these essays, including Joshua, Denise, Conner, David, Benjamin, Zach, Timmi, Patty, Katie, Colin, Alisa, Emilio, Eliza, Ari, Lindsey, and many, many others, including my family.

And to Karah, whom I love.

KYLAN RICE lives in North Carolina. His writing has been published in a variety of literary journals, including *Denver Quarterly*, *Kenyon Review*, *Tupelo Quarterly*, and *West Branch*, among others. He studied poetry at Colorado State University and UNC-Chapel Hill, and has served as editor-in-chief for *The Carolina Quarterly*.

Made in the USA
Middletown, DE
10 April 2021

Made in the USA
Middletown, DE
10 April 2021